LIFE
in
SMALL BITES

By James G. Yarbrough, Jr.

First Edition
November 2012

"Standard Operating Procedures"

Today is the last day of the first of your life.
Today is the first day of the rest of your life.

- Anonymous

The wisdom of the wise and
the experience of the ages
are perpetuated by quotations.

- Benjamin Disraeli

Thank you again for purchasing this compilation of aphorisms.

A portion of the revenue received will be donated
to two of my favorite charities:

If you would like to learn more about these two great organizations,
please visit their websites at:

www.habitat.org

www.operationsmile.org

DEDICATION

To my mentors and coaches, my Mom and Dad, Dorothy Ellen and James Sr.

To my children, Robin, George, and Gary, who are my continuous sources of inspiration, pride, and hope.

To my wife, Marlena, who never fails to remind me to live the "Small Bites" that I preach.

To all of the Doers:

> *Good intentions only provide the drive. It is the "driving" that gets us where we want to be.*

Contents

Poems & Musings

Introduction

It always begins with: "Let me tell you a story..." When I was young, my father was a US Army officer. Thankfully, he had strict requirements about respect for elders and authority, personal grooming, decorum, and manners—especially table manners. Practicing these standards has served me well throughout my life.

When I became a parent, I wanted to pass on the teachings that worked for me. Yet as a father guiding my children's development, I admit that instilling proper table manners was challenging at times—"Elbows off the table", "chew with your mouth closed", "only put *small bites* in your mouth" were all endless refrains.

I often took advantage of mealtimes to dispense pedantic morsels—my "small bites" of guidance, insights, or philosophy. While many of these "small bites" were taken from my own experience and inspiration, most came from the borrowed and appreciated wisdom of others, especially my father. My aim was to provide instructions for establishing personal integrity, personal development, and social responsibility.

In spite of my sometimes reluctant audience, some things must have stuck.

I am very proud of my children, who they are, and what they have accomplished. My children are kind, enthusiastic, and compassionate people. They are living lives of integrity and contributing to their communities. In compiling this compendium of aphorisms and quotations, I not only honor my father, I proudly recognize the responsible adults that my children have become.

Before I was a parent, I was a pilot, two seemingly unrelated roles. The lessons I learned from being a pilot in planning, prioritizing, focus, responsibility, and courage certainly benefited my appreciation and performance of being a parent. Likewise, if I were ever to return to the cockpit, I know that my experience as a parent, given all the complexities of communication, guidance, support, education, and decision-making, would make me a better pilot and flight crew member.

I am proud of the time I served as an US Air Force pilot. The skills and risk required of pilots demand great discipline to learn and apply knowledge, judgment, focused attention, courage, and constantly correcting actions. For me, to "make ideas stick" I often make an association with the discipline and actions required in piloting an aircraft. I relate insights, activities, and destinations with required Standard Operating Procedures (SOP) and flight terms.

In this compilation, I have categorized quotes and passages under a general subject heading. I have also associated a flight term with each heading that I deem relevant to the subject matter.

In promoting ideas related to human relationships and personal growth, I did not want to come across as too "spacey". I wanted to establish some connection with things requiring order and discipline. Personal development guides are all too often dismissed as being "fluff". As a pilot and businessman, I have a tendency to ignore the fluff and focus on the core actionable principles.

Pilots must memorize and understand many bits (*small bites*) of information about physics, weather, aeronautical principles, and the technical details and flight characteristics of their aircraft. To make these *small bites* relevant, they must be integrated into a coherent understandable and actionable framework. Also one's actionable and effective framework requires developing good judgment—when to act and when not to, remembering that the superior pilot is one who uses his superior judgment to avoid using his superior skill. My *Small Bites* are selected bits of Wisdom to develop Judgment that leads to Action.

Coming out of the hangar, I would like to share one of my favorite poems, a favorite of many pilots. This poem is a lyrical composite of Courage, Attitude, Goals, Action, and Spirit. I first memorized it when I got my Wings as a jet pilot. In the many years since, I often recite the poem when I feel, or need to feel, inspired.

High Flight

Oh! I have slipped the surly bonds of Earth
And danced the skies on laughter-silvered wings;
Sunward I've climbed, and joined the tumbling mirth
Of sun-split clouds, — and done a hundred things
You have not dreamed of — wheeled and soared and swung
High in the sunlit silence. Hov'ring there,
I've chased the shouting wind along, and flung
My eager craft through footless halls of air. . . .
Up, up the long, delirious burning blue
I've topped the wind-swept heights with easy grace
Where never lark, or ever eagle flew —
And, while with silent, lifting mind I've trod
The high untrespassed sanctity of space,
Put out my hand, and touched the face of God.

- John Gillespie Magee, Jr

For your additional appreciation, you can hear this special poem recited while viewing a video of a USAF T-38 Talon "dancing the skies". The T-38 was the sleek supersonic jet used in the mid-60's through 80's for training pilots. It was a beautiful aircraft and had jaw-dropping performance. This video was used as the sign-off for KSAT TV station of San Antonio, Texas in the 70's and 80's.

Please visit the URL below for this video:

http://bit.ly/tiFvuk

Thank You Again

Thank you again for letting me share these *Small Bites* with you in honoring my parents. Hopefully, you will have discovered useful wisdom, guidance, and potential power in many of them. As appropriate, I hope that you will share these with your children, relatives, friends, and colleagues.

Please assist me in correcting any mistakes you find in misquoting or incorrectly identifying an author. I am also eager to receive your suggestions for quotations that we should add to our compendium. With your help, we may compile a *Small Bites* 4.0++.

You can contact me at

jim@lifeinsmallbites.com

or through my website

www.lifeinsmallbites.com

In this full version, my *Small Bites* are grouped into the following subjects, my selected analogous pilot terms are shown in brackets:

GENERAL WISDOM   (Standard Operating Procedures)

SELF-KNOWLEDGE   (Operations Manual)

EDUCATION   (Flight Planning)

GOALS   (Mission)

ATTITUDE   (Mission Driven)

RESPONSIBILITY   (Duty)

ACTION   (After-Burners)

COURAGE   (Tailwind)

ADVERSITY   (Turbulence - Emergency Procedures)

LEADERSHIP & MANAGEMENT   (Formation Flying)

SUCCESS   (Mission Accomplished)

FAMILY & FRIENDS   (Air Crew)

SERVICE   (Crew Care)

THANKFULNESS   (Final Approach)

SPIRIT   (Refueling)

I have found that in chewing these *Small Bites* from General Wisdom (SOP), to Goals (Mission), to Responsibility (Duty), to Courage (Tailwind), through to Spirit (Refueling), it has provided me with an actionable framework.

Thank You

Thank you for letting me share these *Small Bites* with you. I trust that you will find some personal value in the passages, a compelling thought, a powerful idea that will guide you to take action. Remember inspiration not backed up by action is like buying a present for a loved one (or yourself) and never giving it. I am confident that you will discover insights and wisdom that will broaden your perspective and help restore your energy, confidence, and commitment to yourself and to others. For this I am grateful.

Many of Dad's entries (mine) may sound cliché to some. For me, they were all spawned by those special moments of "so this is how it is."

If imitation is the sincerest form of flattery, then using and sharing these morsels of wisdom must also rate pretty high.

The insights in *Small Bites* are gleaned from the wisdom of people professing their spiritual practice as Christians, Buddhists, Taoists, Jews, and Muslims. Their wisdom of how to act, succeed, serve, and treat each other transcends their differences.

Question:

How can we create a healthful pandemic of shared wisdom which acknowledges, respects, and allows these religious/philosophical differences while building on these tested universal principles?

Small Bites can become viral passages to supplant negative thinking, negative beliefs, and negative actions with these tested bits of wisdom. Incorporating the wisdom in our own lives through reflected intention and action is the start.

Effective sharing with others by "walking the talk" is the only meaningful game in life. Our responsibility is to live ever more effectively and share our dreams— remembering,

If it is to be, it's up to me.

So here, for your consideration and inspiration are some morsels or *Small Bites*, a few of mine as well as the wisdom of others. Please take these gifts, these *Small Bites*, chew, savor, and live them freely.

Let us begin.

Chapter 1

PRE-FLIGHT

Having been a student and an avid reader of personal development literature for many years, I greatly appreciate the guidance I have received from the teachings of others. I have devoured and assimilated the wisdom and insights from countless books, tapes, videos, DVDs, and courses, and I'm always hungry for more.

Some well-meaning friends have told me, "Enough! Use what you've already learned." Their comments have merit in that, if we don't do what we know, then we don't really know. Therefore, my challenge is to continually work to act in accordance with the teachings as I learn them.

My living spaces were often cluttered with the books, tapes, videos, DVDs, and remnants of these personal development courses. Although my overflowing library felt like a repository of useful information and wisdom, the contents were not as readily accessible as I would have liked. I found that if I distilled the insights into memorable "sound bites", they became more readily available for providing inspiration and direction, often for dealing with the unexpected challenges of life. I began collecting these distillations and even authoring my own. These became my own "small bites".

1

At the dinner table, "don't bite off more than you can chew" meant "keep your intake manageable". In this era of information overload, this is a useful adage for most things. However, it doesn't imply that we shouldn't aim high and work to exceed expectations. Rather, it tells us to discriminate the chewable from the unnecessary—reduce overload and act first on the priorities offering the greatest return.

Small Bites is a categorized compilation of aphorisms and poems that served as inspirational guides and instructions to me and which I shared with my children.

Small Bites is far from exhaustive. I included only those passages which inspired a personal, "Ah so...Yes, but of course", prodding useful reflection, or new, or renewed awareness. Distilling personal "aha's" into words has helped me refine and share the insights. Wherever relevant, I've worked to link passages with related messages.

Unlike food or most nutritional supplements which provide temporary energy benefit, *Small Bites*, consumed properly, have "staying power" with no "sell-by" dates. These bites can be self-regenerating and sustaining fuel energizing you to take timely appropriate actions to move toward your goals.

To unleash the potential energy you must convert the "aha's"—your personal insights, to "action steps". You start by capturing and grounding your insights by writing them down and relating the wisdom to your current reality of where you are and where you want to go. As Naveed Peerzade of IM Protégé said,

> *Simply reading or thinking them keeps them floating around in the realm of possibilities to be tackled "some day." "Some day", the procrastinator's crutch, too often never comes.*

To encourage you to capture your insights, I have included at the end of each chapter a blank page with the heading, "Notes—Record some of your insights and decisions here:"

Life is not like chapters in a text book where one subject ends and the next begins. There are many "chapters of experience" with some impactful isolated events and relationships. Yet these flow from one to another. All our experiences and relationships build on our previous ones. Our mission is to take this collage, this gathering of *small bites* of insights and wisdom, and re-order them to support our growth and success.

Like a car at night, you can only see as far ahead as is being illuminated by your headlights. These wise passages can greatly extend your illuminating beams. I recommend that you allow these quotations to become conversations with yourself and in this manner, allow these *Small Bites* to extend your personal insights beyond your own experience.

A personal note: The first book of aphorisms that I collected and packaged as a high school graduation gift for my oldest son was titled, "Never Pass Up A Chance To Pee". I had learned the wisdom of not putting off what can, and should, be done now, and if not, becomes a negative distraction later. Timely appropriate action is the key.

After collecting and categorizing these aphorisms and quotations for years, this insight was reinforced and it became ever more evident that aside from General Wisdom and Self Knowledge, the most effective catalysts for personal development and leadership progress were those related to taking Action.

It is said that if you can change your thinking, you can change your life. This is only the first step. Life changes only occur when we change our "doing."

If I Could Give You Anything

The following passage was the first entry in the original "*Small Bites*" booklet that I presented to my son, Gary, at his high school graduation.

Michael Josephson, of the Josephson Foundation on Ethics, wrote the following to his daughter on the occasion of her Bat Mitzvah. I adapted it for my son.

If I Could Give You Anything
If I could give you anything, anything at all,
I would give you all the things the poets write about—deep blue skies, pure white clouds, warm sunshine, cool breezes, stunning sunsets, glorious rainbows, and grand waterfalls.
I would give you something to smile about every day.
I would surround you with true friends to share your joys, comfort you through tough times, and bring out the best in you.
I would give you great teachers to fill your mind with wondrous facts, unanswered questions, and a love for learning.
I would give you the wisdom to know your heart and the courage to follow it.
I would fill your days with carefree play and meaningful work.
I would give you challenges worthy of your talents and achievements worthy of your pride.
I would fill your heart with gratitude and teach it to forgive.
I would give you genuine self-confidence, fearless enthusiasm, and grand expectations.
I would give you a life filled with hugs, laughter, love, and the wisdom to be happy.
And when you are ready, I would give you a woman worthy to be your lifelong partner and the mother of your children.
And I would give you a son as good as you.
Sadly, I don't have the power to give you all these things.
But I can remind you that you have the power within you to find, make, and keep all the things I wish for you.

- Michael Josephson

Suggestions For Using Small Bites

If it's to be, it's up to me.

Integrate these passages, when appropriate, in your conversation to so-
lidify your commitment to act on insights and share these gifts with others. Personal power is also found in having these conversations with
yourself. I have found increased relevance and energy by personalizing
these passages. I suggest the following:

1. Convert all of the second or third person "You", "One", or "They" in
   every *Small Bite* passage to the first person "I", "Me", "We", or "Us".
2. Chew and digest a little at a time. Select one to three passages each
   day and commit to memory.

This regimen will help you build up your personal repertoire of wisdom
by 10 to 20 *Small Bites* every week, creating and stimulating neural path-
ways and encouraging taking responsible action. In time, these path-
ways will become habits—SOP to guide and support you.

When you memorize your selected *Small Bites*, keep a pen and paper
handy. Personal insights and ideas to act on should be captured on paper
as you begin to create your own "small bites". The author/coach John
C. Maxwell reminds us that most often ideas have a short shelf-life and
must be captured before they expire.

Let me ask you a question. Why would you want to spend time with
these passages if you didn't want to improve the quality of your life and
those of your loved ones?

The quality of your life is largely dependent on the quality of your actions. The directions of your actions are generally based on your answers to your own questions. If you are asking the wrong questions, the
answers may not matter, but the actions will.

A suggested start is to improve the quality of your questions. I suggest three to support you in framing improved responses to insights gained from *Small Bites.*

3 A's

As you read and consider each Small Bite, ask yourself:

1. What *Awareness* is stimulated?
2. How does this *Apply* to me?
3. What *Action* will I take today to put insight to practice?

As an encouragement, I have placed the reminder "3 A's?" at the bottom of each page.

Let me give you another challenge and a gift:

The science of linguistics contends that communication is only 7% in the words. 38% of the meaning is transmitted through the tone or voice qualities, and 55% is based on the physiology with which the message of the words is conveyed.

Therefore, unleash the power of these *Small Bites* by standing and reciting these passages aloud. Use your voice. Use your body. Connect the message to your intentions through animated expression and thereby lift the impact above mere reflective reading.

That's the challenge. Receiving the gift is up to you.

Notes
Record some of your own insights and decisions here

For wisdom is more precious than rubies,
and nothing you desire can compare with her.

- The Proverbs 8: 11

Chapter II

GENERAL WISDOM
(Standard Operating Procedures)

In 1800, the world's population was 900 million.

Today, it is over 7 billion.

200 years ago:

- 2 % of our earth's people lived in cities.
  Today, it is more than 51 %.
- 95 % depended on agriculture for livelihood.
  Today, it is less than 9 %.
- 20 % could read or write.
  Today, global literacy is estimated to be greater than 84 %.

The insights from some of the contributors in this book date back more than 2,000 years ago, yet the inherent wisdom is still fully applicable, based on principles and values that transcend cultures, genders, and ages.

Tomorrow will find us ever more connected, ever more urban, ever more challenged to keep pace with technological, social, and economic changes. Although responses to these challenges must necessarily accommodate these changes, my experience is that, these timeless declared principles and values transcend the ages and can transform current and future challenges.

Standard Operating Procedures (SOP)

Always watch your "six". (180 degrees behind you)

- Anonymous

Fly the Wind.

- Anonymous

To build a strong character you must:

- practice Patience when others are hurried
- practice Focus when others lack commitment
- practice Self-control when others are frazzled
- practice Gratitude when others are complaining
- practice Generosity when others are selfish
- practice Getting-up when others are content to lie about.

- Dad

Rotary International Four-Way Test of the things we think, say or do:

1. Is it the truth?

2. Is it fair to all concerned?

3. Will it build goodwill and better friendships?

4. Will it be beneficial to all concerned?

3 A's?

The Paradoxical Commandments

People may be illogical, unreasonable, and self-centered.
Love them anyway.

When you do good, people may accuse you of selfish ulterior motives.
Do good anyway.

When you are successful, you may win false friends and true enemies.
Succeed anyway.

The good you do today may be forgotten tomorrow.
Do good anyway.

Honesty and frankness may make you vulnerable.
Be honest and frank anyway.

The biggest men and women with the biggest ideas may be shot down
by the smallest men and women with the smallest minds.
Think big anyway.

People favor underdogs but follow only top dogs.
Fight for a few underdogs anyway.

What you spend years building may be destroyed overnight.
Build anyway.

People really need help but may attack you if you do help them.
Help people anyway.

Give the world the best you have and you may still get kicked in the
teeth.
Give the world the best you have anyway.

- Kent M. Keith

When Life kicks you in the teeth you have two choices:
- Wallow in self-pity and give-up, or
- Get-up and Fight!

- Dad

Life is not fair. Life just "is". Your Job is to take the what "is" and make it better.

- Dad

In the game of life, surrender is not an option.

- Dad

Take action to insure that Not Now's do not become Never Will's.
- Dad

Do what you know to do, only more of it.
Don't do what you know not to do.

- Dad

There is no future in the past.

- Ken Lambert

You may not be able to control a bird from flying over your head, but you sure as heck can stop it from building a nest in it.
- Stephen Pierce

No problem can be solved from the same level of consciousness that created it.

- Albert Einstein

Honesty is the first chapter in the book of wisdom.

- Thomas Jefferson

Whatever you are, be a good one.

- Abraham Lincoln

Where you stand depends on where you sit.

- Nelson Mandela

Too soon we breast the tape, too late we learn the joy is in the running.

- Anonymous

A man cannot directly choose his circumstances, but he can choose his thoughts, and so indirectly, yet surely, shape his circumstances.

- Napoleon Hill

The only thing that you can control is the "meaning" you give to something.

- Anthony Robbins

Life ends when you stop Dreaming,
Hope ends when you stop Believing,
Love ends when you stop Caring,
Friendship ends when you stop Sharing.

- Anonymous

Happy Wife. Happy Life.

- Anonymous

The person who says it cannot be done should not interrupt the person who is doing it.

- Dad

As You improve the World improves.

- Anonymous

_____ is the thing that keeps on giving.
(Fill in the blank with any of the following:
  - Gratitude
  - Discipline
  - Courage
  - Integrity
  - Service
  - Humor

The greatest thing in this world is not so much where we stand as in what direction we are moving.

- Johann Wolfgang von Goethe

3 A's?

The greatest arrogance and ignorance is to reject and or criticize something that you know nothing about.

- Dad

PAUSE…

Save your negative comments.
Save your judgments.
Save your criticisms.

More favorable consequences are wrought from giving positive silent support than ego-related unsolicited advice.

- Dad

Blaming others makes consequential self-deception and irresponsibility take deeper root.

- Dad

Things never to lose:
- *Your Passport*
- *Your Honor*
- *Your Sense of Humor*

- Dad

A Sense of Humor is just Common Sense, Dancing.

- Clive James
*from the book **Dancing***

3 A's?

Do not compare yourself to others – there will always be greater and lesser persons than yourself.

- Max Ehrmann

Be yourself, everyone else is taken!

- Oscar Wilde

If you cannot get a compliment any other way, pay yourself one.

- Mark Twain

Happiness is when what you think, what you say, and what you do are in harmony.

- Mahatma Gandhi

Remember the good thing about the Future is that it only comes one day at a time.

- Abraham Lincoln

It makes sense to begin "forever" today, not tomorrow.

- Anonymous

Whoever undertakes to set himself up as a judge of Truth and Knowledge is shipwrecked by the laughter of the gods.

- Albert Einstein

The time is always right to do the right thing.
                                        - Martin Luther King, Jr.

Always leave a place better than you found it.
                                        - Dad

No one ever went broke saving money.
                                        - J. Jackson Brown

Live without pretending.
Love without depending.
Listen without defending.
Speak without offending.

                                        - Michael Josephson

Heaven and Earth are like a set of bellows. Although empty, they are endlessly productive. The more you work them, the more they produce.

The mouth, on the other hand, becomes exhausted if you talk too much. Often better to keep your thoughts inside you.
                                        - Taoist saying

Do not float a battleship of words around a rowboat of thought.
                                        - Phil Donahue

3 A's?   17

Railing about something eminently unimportant has conse-quences beyond being a duplicitous waste of energy.

- Dan Barry

Remember not only to say the right thing in the right place, but far more difficult still, to leave unsaid the wrong thing at the tempting moment.

- Winston Churchill

Before you criticize someone, you should walk a mile in their shoes. That way when you criticize them you will be a mile away and you will have their shoes.

- Michael Josephson

Communication is the Response you get.

- Marshall Thurber

A virtuous person promotes agreement.
A person without virtue promotes blame.

- Tao

Yesterday is a dream. Tomorrow is a vision. But today, well lived, makes every yesterday a dream of happiness and every tomor-row a vision of hope.

- Anonymous

Uncertainty is the only certainty there is, and knowing how to live with insecurity is the only security.

- *John Allen Paulos*

Age is an issue of mind over matter. If you don't mind, it doesn't matter.

- *Mark Twain*

Wisdom is always an overmatch for strength.

- *Phil Jackson*

Learn to express rather than impress. Expressing evokes a "me-too" attitude while impressing evokes a "so-what" attitude.

- *James Rohn*

Wisdom consists not so much in knowing what to do in the ultimate as in knowing what to do next.

- *Herbert Hoover*

Hearing is one of the body's five senses. But listening is an art.

- *Frank Tyger*

A "no" uttered from deepest conviction is better and greater than a "yes" merely uttered to please, or what is worse, to avoid trouble.

- *Mahatma Gandhi*

It is the nature of the wise to resist pleasures, but the foolish to be a slave to them.

- Epictetus

You can tell whether a man is clever by his answers.
You can tell whether a man is wise by his questions.

- Naguib Mahfouz

When you're arguing with a fool, make sure he isn't doing the same thing.

- Anonymous

Yesterday is a "Cancelled Check"
Tomorrow is a "Promissory Note"
Today is "Cash-in-Hand".

- Stephen Pierce

Someone once said:
-- What goes around comes around.
-- Work like you don't need the money.
-- Love like you've never been hurt.
-- Dance like nobody's watching.
-- Sing like nobody's listening.
-- Live like it's Heaven on earth.

- Anonymous

3 A's?

When wealth is lost, nothing is lost;
When health is lost, something is lost;
When character is lost, all is lost!

- German Proverb

If they can make penicillin out of mouldy bread, they can sure make something out of you.

- Muhammad Ali

Manifest plainness,
Embrace simplicity,
Reduce selfishness,
Have few desires.

– Lao-Tzu,

Conduct is what we do; character is what we are. Character is the root of the tree; conduct is the fruit it bears.

- E. M. Bounds

There is no pillow so soft as a clear conscience.

- French proverb

It is not what we read, but what we remember that makes us learned. It is not what we intend but what we do that makes us useful. And, it is not a few faint wishes but a lifelong struggle that makes us valiant.

- Henry Ward Beecher

To your enemy, forgiveness
To an opponent, tolerance
To a friend, your heart
To a customer, service
To all, charity
To every child, a good example
To yourself, respect

- Oren Arnold

Just as treasures are uncovered from the earth, so virtue appears from good deeds, and wisdom appears from a pure and peaceful mind. To walk safely through the maze of human life, one needs the light of wisdom and the guidance of virtue.

- Gautama Buddha

Life is like a ten-speed bike. Most of us have gears we never use.

- Charles Schultz

You cannot shake hands with a clenched fist.

- Mahatma Gandhi

The Weak can never forgive. Forgiveness is the attribute of the Strong.

- Mahatma Gandhi

3 A's?

One Day At A Time

There are two days in every week about which we should not worry--two days that should be kept free from fear and appre-hension.

One of these days is yesterday with its mistakes and cares, faults and blunders, aches and pains. Yesterday has passed forever be-yond our control. All the money in the world cannot bring back yesterday. We cannot undo a single act we performed. We cannot erase a single word we said. Yesterday is gone!

The other day we should not worry about is tomorrow. Tomor-row's sun will rise, whether in splendor or behind a mask of clouds. Until it does, we have no stake in tomorrow. It is yet unborn.

This leaves only one day: today. It is when we add the burdens of two eternities - yesterday and tomorrow that we break down.

It is not necessarily the experience of today that disturbs one's peace of mind. It is often the bitterness for something that hap-pened yesterday and the dread of what tomorrow may bring.

Let us therefore live one day at a time.

- Jennifer Kritsh

One's philosophy is not best expressed in words; it is expressed in the choices one makes. In the long run, we shape our lives and we shape ourselves. And, the choices we make are ultimately our own responsibility.

- Eleanor Roosevelt

Hold on to what is Good,
Even if it is a handful of earth.

Hold on to what you Believe,
Even if it is a tree which stands by itself.

Hold on to what you must Do,
Even if it is a long way from here.

Hold on to Life,
Even if it is easier to let go.

Hold on to my Hand,
Even when I have gone away from you.

- Pueblo Verse

Trust is the water that all relationships swim in.

- George Dom

Our vision is:

Love - through Service to others
Peace – through Reconciliation
Joy – through generous Hospitality.

- Koinonia Mission

3 A's?

Virtues like honesty, love, compassion, and service create a moral gravity that attracts opportunities, rewarding relationships, and an enduring peace of mind that only comes to those who live worthy lives.

– Michael Josephson

You cannot make money or muscles and excuses at the same time.

- Stephen Pierce

In the Workplace and in Life, you get the behavior that you reward.

- Dad

In the end the love you take is equal to the love you make.

- The Beatles

Give so much time to improve yourself that you have no time to criticize others.

- Christian Larson

Our ultimate freedom is the right and power to decide how anybody or anything outside ourselves will affect us.

- Stephen Covey

To know how to do something is skill.
To know why to do something is wisdom.
To know when to do something is judgment.
To know to strive to do your best is dedication.
To do it for the benefit of others is compassion.
To get the job done is achievement.
To do this quietly is humility.
To get others to do all of these things willingly is leadership.

- Anonymous

Coach John Wooden's 7 Point Creed

1. To Your Own self be True
2. Help Others
3. Make Each Day your Masterpiece
4. Make Friendship a Fine Art
5. Drink Deeply from Good Books
6. Build a Shelter Against a Rainy Day
7. Give Thanks for your Blessings and Ask for Guidance Every Day

Nine requisites for contented living:

1. Health enough to make work a pleasure
2. Wealth enough to support your needs
3. Strength to battle with difficulties and overcome them
4. Grace enough to confess your sins and forsake them
5. Patience enough to toil until some good is accomplished
6. Charity enough to see some good in your neighbor
7. Love enough to move you to be useful to others
8. Faith enough to make real the things of God
9. Hope enough to remove all anxious fears concerning the future

- Johann Wolfgang von Goethe

3 A's?

Don't judge each day by the harvest you reap, but by the seeds you plant.

- Robert Louis Stevenson

If you follow no other truth, follow the truth that within your being is called Joy. If you follow that, you're always going to be right where you need to be, and you will always have life within your being.

- Sheradon Bryce

Life is short. Bend the rules. Forgive quickly. Love truly. Laugh uncontrollably. Be grateful daily. And never regret anything that made you smile!

- Anonymous

People are like stained-glass windows. They sparkle and shine when the sun is out, but when the darkness sets in; their true beauty is revealed only if there is a light from within.

– Elizabeth Kübler-Ross

Desiderata

Go placidly amid the noise and the haste,
and remember what peace there may be in silence.

As far as possible, without surrender,
be on good terms with all persons.

Speak your truth quietly and clearly,
and listen to others,
even to the dull and the ignorant;
they too have their story.

Avoid loud and aggressive persons;
they are vexatious to the spirit.

If you compare yourself with others,
you may become vain or bitter,
for always there will be greater and lesser persons than yourself.

Enjoy your achievements as well as your plans.
Keep interested in your own career, however humble;
it is a real possession in the changing fortunes of time.

Exercise caution in your business affairs,
for the world is full of trickery,
but let this not blind you to what virtue there is.
Many persons strive for high ideals,
and everywhere life is full of heroism.

Be yourself.
Especially do not feign affection.

Neither be cynical about love,
for in the face of all aridity and disenchantment
it is as perennial as the grass.

Take kindly the counsel of the years,
gracefully surrendering the things of youth.

Nurture strength of spirit to shield you in sudden misfortune,
but do not distress yourself with dark imaginings.
Many fears are born of fatigue and loneliness.

Beyond a wholesome discipline,
be gentle with yourself.

You are a child of the universe
no less than the trees and the stars;
you have a right to be here.
And whether or not it is clear to you,
no doubt the universe is unfolding as it should.
Therefore be at peace with God,
whatever you conceive Him to be.

And whatever your labors and aspirations,
in the noisy confusion of life,
keep peace in your soul.

With all its sham, drudgery, and broken dreams,
it is still a beautiful world.
Be cheerful.
Strive to be happy.

- Max Ehrmann

Believe In Your Heart

Believe in your heart that something wonderful is about to happen.

Love your life.

Believe in your own powers, and your own potential,
and in your own innate goodness.

Wake every morning with the awe of just being alive.

Discover each day the magnificent, awesome beauty in the world.

Explore and embrace life in yourself and in everyone you see each day.

Reach within to find your own specialness.

Amaze yourself and rouse those around you to the potential of each new day.

Don't be afraid to admit that you are less than perfect;
this is the essence of your humanity.

Let those who love you help you.

Trust enough to be able to take.

Look with hope to the horizon of today, for today is all we truly have.

Live this day well.

Let a little sun out as well as in.

Create your own rainbows.

Be open to all your possibilities; all possibilities and Miracles.

Always believe in Miracles.

- Anonymous

Everyone wants to be appreciated.
So, if you appreciate someone, don't keep it a secret.

- Mary Kay Ash

Every day is a journey, and the journey itself is home.

- Matsuo Basho

Lies, deceptions and broken promises don't remove stones from the top of the tower they imperil the foundation by taking them from the bottom.

- Michael Josephson

From the errors of others, a wise man corrects his own.

- Publilius Syrus

Put your future in good hands. Your own.

- Mark Victor Hansen

You can't talk yourself out of a problem you behaved yourself into.

- Stephen Covey

Don't approach a goat from the front, a horse from the back, or a fool from any side.

- Jewish proverb

3 A's?

One evening an old man told his grandson about a battle that goes on inside all people. He said, "My son, there is a battle between two 'wolves' inside us all.

"One is Evil. It is anger, envy, jealousy, sorrow, regret, greed, arrogance, self-pity, guilt, resentment, inferiority, lies, false pride, superiority, and ego.

"The other is Good. It is joy, peace, love, hope, serenity, humility, kindness, benevolence, empathy, generosity, truth, compassion and faith."

The grandson thought about it for a minute and then asked his grandfather: "Which wolf wins?"

The old man simply replied, "The one you feed..."

- Anonymous

Don't taunt the alligator until after you've crossed the creek.

- Dan Rather

3 A's?

Notes

Record some of your own insights and decisions here

Know Thyself.

- Inscription at Temple of Apollo at Adelphi

Let him that would move the world first move himself.

- Socrates

Chapter III

SELF-KNOWLEDGE
(Operations Manual)

The essential meaning and purpose of life is to become the best version of yourself.
                                                                    - Mathew Kelly

You are today where your thoughts have brought you;
You will be tomorrow where your thoughts take you.
                                                                    - James Allen

Our brain is sometimes compared to a computer in that you can only take out what you put in. Our brains are infinitely more complex than a computer and are capable of creative thought, yet the comparison has some merit in that it is a strong caution to be wary of the "garbage in, garbage out" syndrome. It is up to us to put in information and concepts that will promote our well-being and success. If we do not do our own programming, someone else will do it for us.

With this in mind I work to supply my Inner Voice with supportive material for positive programming. I know that my Inner Voice, the good one that knows and wants the best for me is like a muscle—it gets stronger with exercise. I must Use it or lose it.

A question that I continually ask my Inner Voice is, "What different attitudes should I program and what actions should I take if I lived to honor the truth that integrity has more value than money, position, or ego?"

I also know that it is important to realize that my Inner Voice is separate from my Ego. Emotions like anger, resentment, pride, or embarrassment are ego-connected and cause me to be self-absorbed. Body hits like these are not signs from my Inner Voice. To hear my Inner Voice clearly I have to get Ego out of the way.

Getting Ego out of the way is a constant challenge for me. Ego always wants to compare my actions and results to others. I work to not let my short-comings define me. I claim that I am my own authority for my self-worth. I affirm that Spirit as speaking through my Inner Voice only wants the best for me and reminds me to be generous with compassion for myself and others.

I have found that compassionate thoughts must become ingrained habits. Coloring and immersing our thoughts with the wisdom of others works to strengthen our Inner Voice. Remember, if you are not doing your own programming, someone will do it for you. The Proverbs caution,

As a man thinketh in his heart, so is he.

As the Roman Emperor and Stoic philosopher, Marcus Aurelius (121 – 180 AD) advised,

Such as they are, thy habitual thoughts, such also will be the character of your mind; for the Soul is dyed by these thoughts.

The Greatest Achievement

The greatest achievement is selflessness.

The greatest worth is self-mastery.

The greatest quality is seeking to serve others.

The greatest precept is continual awareness.

The greatest medicine is the emptiness of everything.

The greatest action is not conforming with the world's ways.

The greatest magic is transmuting the passions.

The greatest generosity is non-attachment.

The greatest goodness is a peaceful mind.

The greatest patience is humility.

The greatest effort is not concerned with results.

The greatest meditation is a mind that lets go.

The greatest wisdom is seeing through appearances.

- Buddhist Wisdom

Each day is planning and preparation for the next. What you become is a result of what you did today.

- Dad

Ability may get you to the top, but it takes character to keep you there.

- John Wooden

Do not allow others' limited perceptions to define you.

- Dad

The only opinion about your dream that really counts is yours. The negative comments of others merely reflect their limitations - not yours.

- Cynthia Kersey

Challenge your own "limiting beliefs" by questioning them. If you begin to question a limiting belief, you automatically weaken it.

- Dad

It is said that 80% of the time people already know where they need help. Practice acting on what you know.

- Dad

Anything that hooks you into emotion can take control of you.

- Dad

3 A's?

To take charge of your emotions and empower more effective actions you must disallow being "bothered". Convert "bother" to empathy.

- Dad

My life is in the hands of any fool that makes me lose my temper.

- Joseph Hunter

Anger is an acid that can do more harm to the vessel in which it is stored than to anything on which it is poured.

- Mark Twain

We are where we are, as we are, because of what we are.

- Earle J. Glade

What we think, we become.

- Gautama Buddha

It ain't what you don't know that gets you into trouble. It's what you know for sure that just ain't so.

- Mark Twain

It's not what you are that holds you back, it's what you think you're not.

- Denis Waitley

Be who you are and say what you feel because those who mind don't matter and those who matter don't mind.

- Dr. Seuss

Self-respect knows no considerations.

- Mohandas Gandhi

I never was what "I used to be" – so it's time to start now.

- Anonymous

Begin to be now what you will be hereafter.

- Saint Jerome

It is not the mountain we conquered, but ourselves.

- Sir Edmund Hillary

We are generally better persuaded by the reasons we discover ourselves than by those given to us by others.

- Blaise Pascal

I went to the woods because I wished to live deliberately, to front only the essential facts of life, and see if I could not learn what it had to teach, and not, when I came to die, discover that I had not lived.

- Henry David Thoreau
from the book **Walden**

Until you make peace with who you are ... you'll never be content with what you have.

- Doris Mortman

Too many people overvalue what they are not and undervalue what they are.

- Malcolm Forbes

You were born an original. Don't die a copy.

- John Mason

The deepest secret is that life is not a process of discovery, but a process of creation. You are not discovering yourself, but creating yourself anew. Seek, therefore, not to find out who you are, seek to determine who you want to be.

- Neale Donald Walsh
from the book **Conversations With God**

Matter derives from Mind,
Not Mind from Matter.

- Tibetan Book of the Great Liberation

Great ideas, it is said, come into the world as gently as doves. Perhaps, then, if we listen attentively, we shall hear amid the uproar of empires and nations a faint flutter of wings, the gentle stirring of life and hope.

- Albert Camus

3 A's?

To be nobody but yourself - in a world which is doing its best, night and day, to make you like everybody else - means to fight the hardest battle which any human being can fight - and never stop fighting.

- E.E. Cummings

We forfeit three-fourths of ourselves in order to be like other people.

- Arthur Schopenhauer

Be yourself. Everyone else is taken.

- Oscar Wilde

Swallow your pride occasionally, it's not fattening.

- Frank Tyger

Let us not look back in anger, nor forward in fear, but around us in awareness.

- Leland Val Vandewall

The cyclone derives its powers from a calm center. So does a person.

- Norman Vincent Peale

Humility does not mean you think less of yourself. It means you think of yourself less.

- Ken Blanchard

3 A's?

Ethics doesn't require us to ignore our self-interests or demand a life of self-sacrifice. It requires that we know the difference between what we want and what we should do.

- Michael Josephson

As human beings, our greatness lies not so much in being able to remake the world ... as in being able to remake ourselves.

- Mahatma Gandhi

The Best Within You

In the name of the best within you, do not sacrifice this world to those who are at its worst. In the name of the values that keep you alive, do not let your vision of man be distorted by the ugly, the cowardly, the mindless in those who have never achieved his title.

Do not lose your knowledge that man's proper estate is an upright posture, an intransigent mind and a step that travels unlimited roads. Do not let your fire go out, spark by irreplaceable spark, in the hopeless swamps of the approximate, the not-quite, the not-yet, the not-at-all.

Do not let the hero in your soul perish, in lonely frustration for the life you deserved, but have never been able to reach. Check your road and the nature of your battle. The world you desired can be won, it exists, it is real, it's yours.

- Ayn Rand
*from **Atlas Shrugged***

The essential meaning and purpose of life is to become the best-version-of-yourself.

- Matthew Kelly

The power of one is above all things the power to believe in yourself. Often well beyond any latent ability previously demonstrated. The mind is the athlete. The body is simply the means it uses.

- Bryce Courtenay

There is no fire like greed,
No crime like hatred,
No sorrow like separation,
No sickness like hunger of heart,
And no joy like the joy of freedom.
Health, contentment and trust are your greatest possessions,
and freedom your greatest joy.
Look within.
Be still.
Free from fear and attachment,
know the sweet joy of living in the Way.

- adapted from the Dhammapada

Imagination is the beginning of Creation.
You Imagine what you Desire,
then Will what you Imagine,
then at last you Create what you Will.

- George Bernard Shaw

3 A's?

You are your deepest driving Desire,
As is your Desire so is your Will,
As is your Will so is your Deed,
As Is your Deed so is your Destiny.
-Therefore your Desire can become your Destiny.
                                    - Upanishads (ancient Vedic text)

What will matter is not what you bought but what you built,
not what you got but what you gave.
What will matter is not your success but your significance.
What will matter is not what you learned but what you taught.
What will matter is every act of integrity, compassion,
courage or sacrifice that enriched, empowered or encouraged
others.
                                    - Michael Josephson

It is only by submerging oneself in the humanity of others that we
know ourselves more fully.
                                    - Christopher Moore

When you realize no one on earth can be like you...that no other
soul may know the beauty, sorrow, light and darkness you alone
are given to see... then you will, at last, be the fearless individual
your Heart of hearts has called you to be.
                                    - Guy Finley

Make no friendship with an angry man and with a furious man
thou shall not go; lest thou learn his ways, and get a snare to thy
soul.
                                    - The Proverbs 22: 24-25

Notes
Record some of your own insights and decisions here

The purpose of education is to know where to go,
to learn what you need to know,
and what to do with it when you find it.

- Ron Hensley

Chapter IV

EDUCATION
(Flight Planning)

You are your own driving engine and you are your own brake.
You determine your own fate. Study well.

- Anonymous

Most parents emphasize the importance of education for their children. As parents, we are concerned that our children will have the knowledge and skills to successfully navigate tomorrow's challenges— providing for themselves financially and socially.

Some of these skills and knowledge can become obsolete in time, some are timeless. For me, knowing how to change spark plugs and adjust a carburetor are now less useful than my learning of mathematics, accounting, finance, team-building, or project management.

Education must be capacity building, like leadership, negotiation competence, presentation skills for instance. Learning about geology, geography, foreign cultures, music, and art has also served me well. The wisdom in *Small Bites* suggests that the purpose of Education is to not only extend one's ability to provide for oneself and one's family, but essential for the full experience and enjoyment of life.

Flight Planning

Life loses its meaning when the learning stops.

- Dad

Man's mind, once stretched by a new idea, never regains its original dimensions.

- Oliver Wendell Holmes

The Mind ages only with disuse. Constant exercise of the Mind keeps it young and agile.

- Dad

Learning is the beginning of wealth. Learning is the beginning of health. Learning is the beginning of spirituality. Searching and learning is where the miracle process all begins.

- Jim Rohn

Learn from yesterday, live for today, hope for tomorrow. The important thing is not to stop questioning.

- Albert Einstein

A mind, like a home, is furnished by its owner, so if one's life is cold and bare he can blame none but himself.

- Louis L'Amour

Education is not the filling of the pail, but the lighting of a fire.
                                        - William Butler Yeats

The purpose of education is to know where to go, to learn what you need to know, and what to do with it when you find it.
                                        - Ron Hensley

Give me six hours to chop down a tree and I will spend the first four sharpening the axe.
                                        - Abraham Lincoln

There are no shortcuts to excellence.
                                        - Anonymous

If they can make penicillin out of moldy bread, they can sure make something out of you.
                                        - Muhammad Ali

You grow up when you won't give up.
                                        - Dad

You can't stop the waves, but you can learn how to surf.
                                        - Anonymous

Anyone who stops learning is old, whether at 20 or 80. Anyone who keeps learning stays young. The greatest thing in life is to keep your mind young.

- Henry Ford

By three methods we may learn wisdom:
First, by reflection, which is noblest;
Second, by imitation, which is easiest; and
Third by experience, which is the bitterest.

- Confucius

The intuitive mind is a sacred gift and the rational mind is a faithful servant. We have created a society that honors the servant and has forgotten the gift.

- Albert Einstein

The mediocre teacher (parent) tells.
The good teacher (parent) explains.
The superior teacher (parent) demonstrates.
The great teacher (parent) inspires.

- William Arthur Ward
* (parenthesis inserts are mine)

Without financial education, your money flows to those who profit most from your financial ignorance.

- Robert Kiyosaki

The doors of wisdom are never shut.

- Benjamin Franklin

Notes

Record some of your own insights and decisions here

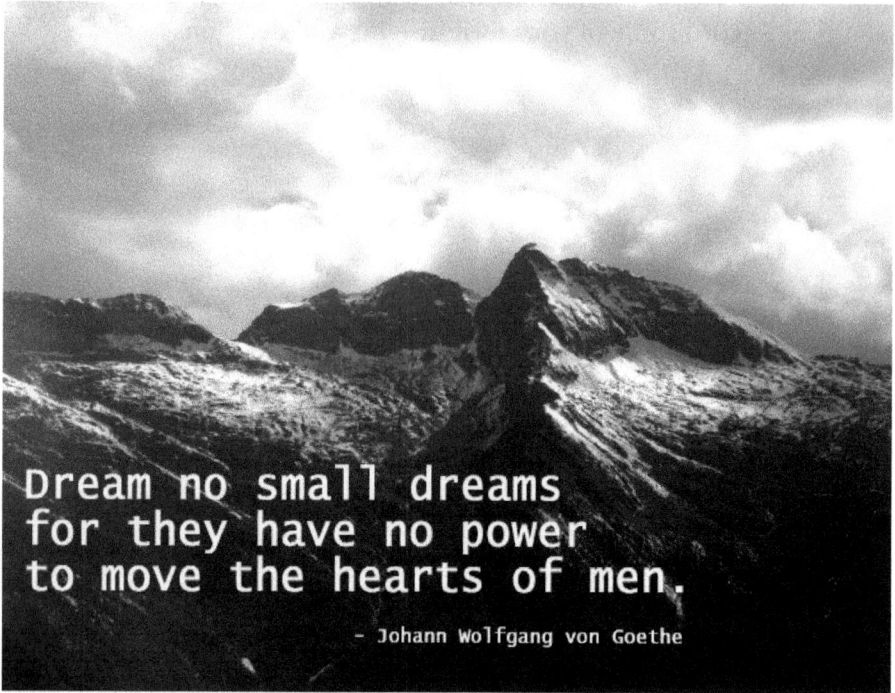

Dream no small dreams
for they have no power
to move the hearts of men.

- Johann Wolfgang von Goethe

Fortune or Fate are not made by waiting for them to come to you.
Plan and aim high.
The likelihood of landing where you want without planning
is like winning a race without running.

- Dad

When you fail to plan you are planning to fail.

- Coach John Wooden

Avoiding failure is not as motivating as chasing achievement.

- Dad

Chapter V

GOALS
(Mission)

Make sure that a large part of your investment strategy is invested in things than cannot erode in value, like education and relationships.

Remember that hope is not a plan. A Goal is hope empowered by faith and structured with a plan. Hope, without these elements, has little energy to inspire or stimulate necessary actions. The more precise the goal and the more detailed the plan, the greater the likelihood that the goal will be achieved.

It's important to have a plan, one based on a considered course of action to get you where you want to go. Equally important is to have a virtual GPS to determine where you are now. An accurate reading of where you are now requires objectively taking stock of your current situation, available resources, and any perceived limitations.

Limitations must be carefully categorized to distinguish between real and just current attitudes. Real limitations should be further categorized to separate the fixed from the malleable. About the only things that are truly fixed are age and time available. All else is conditional and subject to improvement. Attitudinal limitations can be severe obstacles, yet so are the ones that are manageable and within our control. As William Ernest Henley's wonderful poem Invictus reminds us,

> *It matters not how strait the gate,*
> *How charged with punishments the scroll,*
>
> *I am the Master of my fate:*
> *I am the Captain of my soul.*

Mission

The right to choose your own path is a divine right – and a responsibility.

- Dad

Someone said, There is no telling how far you have to run when chasing a dream… – the "Catching" is in the "Chasing".

- Dad

Go big or go home. Because it's true. What do you have to lose?
- Eliza Dushku

Never let the odds keep you from pursuing what you know in your heart that you were meant to do.

- Sachel Paige

Life without meaning is the torture of restlessness and vague desire.
It is a boat longing for the sea and yet afraid.

- Edgar Lee Masters

Without Vision people perish.

- Anonymous

3 A's?

"Why not?" – is a slogan for an interesting life.

- Mason Cooley

A winner concentrates on that which is goal-achieving rather than tension-relieving.

- Denis Waitley

Some say, "All good things must end." It is more useful to view and act on the "winding down" as opportunities for new beginnings.

- Dad

If you don't set a baseline standard for what you'll accept in life, you'll find it's easy to slip into behaviors and attitudes or a quality of life that's far below what you deserve.

- Anthony Robbins

Setting a goal is not the main thing. It is deciding how you will go about achieving it and staying with that plan.

- Tom Landry

Commitments are made in concrete.
Plans are made in sand.

- Anonymous

If you build it, they will come.

- Field of Dreams

In the long run, men hit only what they aim at. Therefore, they had better aim at something high.

- Henry David Thoreau

The only sin in life is low aim.

- Morris Wolff

A man begins cutting his wisdom teeth the first time he bites off more than he can chew.

- Herb Caen

Be the change that you want to see in the world.

- Mohandas Gandhi

Setting goals is the first step in turning the invisible into the visible.

- Anthony Robbins

Obstacles are those frightful things you see when you take your eyes off your goal.

- Henry Ford

To achieve great things, two things are needed; a plan, and not quite enough time.

- Leonard Bernstein

3 A's?

Your present circumstance should not unnecessarily influence or limit your thinking or decision-making. Your future depends on taking action toward where you want to be regardless of where you currently are.

- Dad

When it is obvious that the goals cannot be reached, don't adjust the goals, adjust the action steps.

- *Confucius*

Make every goal clear, specific, measurable, and time-bounded.
- *Brian Tracy*

Perseverance is not a long race; it is many short races one after the other.

- *Walter Elliot*

In life, as in football, you won't go far unless you know where the goalposts are.

- *Arnold H. Glasgow*

Your own words are the bricks and mortar of the dreams you want to realize. Your words are the greatest power you have. The words you choose and use establish the life you experience.

- *Sonia Choquette*

3 A's?

I am not competing with anyone else. I am competing with what I am capable of.

- Michael Jordan

You can only become truly accomplished at something you love. Don't make money your goal. Instead, pursue the things you love doing, and then do them so well that people can't take their eyes off you.

- Maya Angelou

Our real duty is always found running in the direction of our worthiest desires.

- Randolph S. Bourne

Cynicism (is) the intellectual cripple's substitute for intelligence.

- Joseph Russell Lynes

The problems of the world cannot possibly be solved by skeptics or cynics whose horizons are limited by obvious realities. We need men and women who can dream of things that never were.

- John F. Kennedy

Early to bed,
Early to rise,
Makes a man
Healthy, Wealthy, and Wise.

- Proverb

3 A's?

Notes
Record some of your own insights and decisions here

Keep your face to the sunshine and you cannot see the shadows.

- Helen Keller

Any fact facing us is not as important as our attitude toward it,
for that determines our success or failure.

- Norman Vincent Peale

Chapter VI

ATTITUDE
(Mission Driven)

Always bear in mind that your own resolution to succeed is more important than any other.

- Abraham Lincoln

The best years of your life are the ones in which you decide your problems are your own. You do not blame them on your mother, the ecology, or the president. You realize that you control your own destiny.

- Albert Ellis

The willingness to see our own errors in judgments, actions, and attitudes is the basis for personal wisdom and offers the seeds for personal growth. As Michael Josephson advised, we are responsible for choosing the attitudes, actions, and reactions that shape our lives. It is this claiming of personal power that puts us in the driver's seat (cockpit).

Continually ask yourself:

- What attitudes am I nurturing?
- What attitudes am I smothering?
- How are these attitudes affecting my outcomes?
- What am I willing to do about it?

Dreams usually precede doing. Our claimed and acted-on attitudes are the fodder for dreaming and doing. Knowing this is not enough. Anthony Robbins coaches us to act our way into feeling. Act as if, that is as if you felt confident, courageous, wise, energetic, successful...

The acting can push out the doubting and negative thinking and replaces them with foundational attitudes for further positive action.

We create positive actions by eliminating our disempowering attitudes. Allowing ourselves to wallow in self-pity from unmet expectations will not drive us toward new activities that create personal and social value.

All pilots are required to memorize and display competence in performing scripted Emergency Procedures (EP's) for times of need. Even before having to perform the EP's, in an actual situation, the attitudes of confidence and control have worked to override the negative attitudes of fear, doubt, and desperation.

Red lights illuminate in the cockpit when something is going awry. How helpful would it be if we instilled internal attitudinal red lights that would glow when we lapse into feeling fear, doubt, or despair? What if we programmed ourselves to trigger countervailing attitudes when we feel the first surges of one of these disempowering attitudes?

   - Doubt to Confidence
   - Fear to Alertness to options
   - Despair to Resilience

Embrace our refrain,

   If it's to be, it's up to me.

Mission Driven

Coach Jim to his players: "N'Gup! - Never Give up!"

- Dad

Never see failure as failure, but only as part of the game you must play to win.

- Dad

ABILITY is what you're capable of doing.
MOTIVATION determines what you do.
ATTITUDE determines how well you do it.

- Lou Holtz

A happy person is not a person in a certain set of circumstances, but rather a person with a certain set of attitudes.

- Hugh Downs

Happiness is a choice. Happiness is not what happens to you; it is how you relate to what happens to you.

- Sean Stephenson

Attitude is more important than the past, than education, than money, than circumstances, than what people do or say. It is more important than appearance, giftedness, or skill.

- Charles Swindoll

It's the repetition of affirmations that leads to belief. And once that belief becomes a deep conviction, things begin to happen.
                                                        - Muhammad Ali

The truest wisdom is a resolute determination.
                                                        - Napoleon Bonaparte

Discipline is the bridge between goals and accomplishment.
                                                        - Jim Rohn

When we cannot change a situation, resolution comes through the way we choose to handle it within ourselves.
                                                        - Captain Gerald Coffee

Make a commitment that tragedies and disappointments become a source of increased patience, strength, and Wisdom.
                                                        - Dad

Let criticism motivate you.

                                                        - Jan Ruhe

Strength does not come from winning. Your struggles develop your strengths. When you go through hardships and decide not to surrender, that is strength.
                                                        - Arnold Schwarzenegger

3 A's?

Always bear in mind that your own resolution to succeed is more important than any other.

- Abraham Lincoln

The will to win, the desire to succeed, the urge to reach your full potential... these are the keys that will unlock the door to personal excellence.

- Confucius

If I had listened to the critics I'd have died drunk in the gutter.

- Anton Chekov

We can throw stones, complain about them, stumble on them, climb over them, or build with them.

- William Arthur Ward

If you're chasing after anything in life with some level of misdirected anger, that very thing will likely get the better of you in the end.

- Diane Armitage

If you can't bite, don't show your teeth.

- Yiddish Proverb

A man can't ride you unless your back is bent.

- Reverend Martin Luther King, Jr.

3 A's?

Don't conclude before you understand. After you understand – don't judge.

- Ann Dunham
(President Barack Obama's mother)

It isn't the mountains ahead to climb that wear you out; it's the pebble in your shoe.

- Muhammad Ali

It takes a strong man to swim against the current; any dead fish will float with it .

- Anonymous

We must all wage an intense, lifelong battle against the constant downward pull. If we relax, the bugs and weeds of negativity will move into the garden and take away everything of value.

- Jim Rohn

I don't believe you have to be better than everybody else. I believe you have to be better than you ever thought you could be.

- Ken Venturi

Don't water your weeds.

- Harvey Mackay

Laughter is the sun that drives Winter from the human face.

- Victor Hugo

3 A's?

You will not be punished for your anger, you will be punished by your anger.

- Gautama Buddha

I will take every opportunity to laugh. Laughter is the music that makes my trouble dance.

- Anonymous

One comes to believe whatever one repeats to oneself sufficiently often, whether the statement is true of false.

- Robert Collier

Fortify your "self-talk" with courageous affirmations and silence the negative chatter.

- Dad

The key to getting started down the path of being remarkable in anything is simply to act with the intention of being remarkable.

- Chad Fowler

Any man's life will be filled with constant and unexpected encouragement if he makes up his mind to do his level best each day.

- Booker T. Washington

Don't let yesterday use up too much of today.

- Will Rogers

Our attitudes control our lives. Attitudes are a secret power working twenty-four hours a day, for good or bad. It is of paramount importance that we know how to harness and control this great force.

- Tom Blandi

In the game of Life even the 50-yardline seats don't interest me. I came to play!

- H. Jackson Brown

The one resolution, which was in my mind long before it took the form of a resolution, is the keynote of my life. It is this, always to regard as mere impertinences of fate the handicaps which were placed upon my life almost at the beginning. I resolved that they should not crush or dwarf my soul, but rather be made to blossom, like Aaron's rod, with flowers.

- Helen Keller

People think I'm disciplined. It is not discipline. It is devotion. There is a great difference.

- Luciano Pavarotti

The difference between the impossible and the possible lies in a person's determination.

- Tommy Lasorda

Strength does not come from physical capacity. It comes from an indomitable will.

- Mohandas Gandhi

3 A's?

Change is never a matter of ability – it's always a matter of motivation.

- Anthony Robbins

Pessimists may be usually right, optimists may be usually wrong, but most great changes were made by optimists.

- Thomas Friedman

As long as you think the problem is out there, that very thought is the problem.

- Stephen Covey

The key that unlocks energy is desire. It's also the key to a long and interesting life. If we expect to create any drive, any real force within ourselves, we have to get excited.

- Earl Nightingale

Be miserable. Or motivate yourself. Whatever has to be done, it's always your choice.

- Dr. Wayne Dyer

Nothing is going to spoil this moment...Imagine making that decision: nothing's going to spoil this moment. Now, imagine making that decision about a relationship, job, day in the week, or... whatever. Imagine applying that idea uniformly in your life.

- Neale Donald Walsch

3 A's?

In the face of unjust criticism we can become bitter or better; upset or understanding; hostile or humble; furious or forgiving.
                                                    - William Arthur Ward

I have always believed, and I still believe, that whatever good or bad fortune may come our way we can always give it meaning and transform it into something of value.
                                                         - Hermann Hesse

The most glorious moments in your life are not the so-called days of success, but rather those days when out of dejection and despair you feel rise in you a challenge to life, and the promise of future accomplishments.
                                                         - Gustave Flaubert

To believe in something, and not to live it, is dishonest.
                                                    - Mohandas Gandhi

Let us not look back in anger, nor forward in fear, but around us in awareness.
                                                - Leland Val Vandewall

It is the love, self-sacrifice, integrity, and courage of ordinary people that confirm the extraordinary human capacity for nobility and prove that cynicism is a deplorable lie.
                                                - Michael Josephson

Although the world is full of suffering, it is also full of the overcoming of it.

- Helen Keller

One of the things I learned the hard way was that it doesn't pay to get discouraged. Keeping busy and making optimism a way of life can restore your faith in yourself.

- Lucille Ball

Living in the past is kind of like living in a coffin...it's totally constraining, and ends up being a lid on your growth...

- Doug Firebaugh

Make it a rule of life never to regret and never to look back. Regret is an appalling waste of energy; you can't build on it, it's only good for wallowing in.

- Katherine Mansfield

Regrets are for losers - unless used to fuel actions toward becoming resourceful. Unchannelled regrets cause losers to become blind to see through the windows to new opportunities.

- Dad

A pessimist is one who makes difficulties of his opportunities, and an optimist is one who makes opportunities of his difficulties.

- Harry Truman

Anger is a wind which blows out the lamp of the mind.
-Robert Green Ingersoll

The will must be stronger than the skill.
- Muhammad Ali

Optimists enrich the present, enhance the future, challenge the improbable and attain the impossible.
- William Arthur Ward

I've learned that you shouldn't go through life with a catcher's mitt on both hands; you need to be able to throw something back.
- Maya Angelou

Any fool can criticize, condemn, and complain but it takes character and self control to be understanding and forgiving.
- Dale Carnegie

Those who are lifting the world upward and onward are those who encourage more than criticize.
– Elizabeth Harrison

Begin Again

One of the best gifts we can give to ourselves is this:
        Begin again.

Begin to see yourself as you were when you were the Happiest
and strongest you've ever been.

Begin to remember what worked for you
(and what worked against you).
And reach to capture the magic again.

Begin to remember how natural it was when you were a child --
To live a lifetime each day.

Begin to forget the baggage you have carried with you for years:
- The problems that don't matter anymore,
- The tears that cried themselves away,
- And the worries that are going to wash away
On the shore of tomorrow's new beginnings.

Tomorrow tells us that in every new day opportunity lies;
And if we will be wise,
We will turn away from the problems of the past
And give the future -- and ourselves -- a chance
To become the best of friends.

Sometimes all it takes is a wish in the heart to let yourself …
        Begin again.

                          - Sapana

Notes
Record some of your own insights and decisions here

If it's to be, it's up to me!

- Anthony Robbins

Chapter VII

RESPONSIBILITY
(Duty)

Consequences result from actions. When you are not getting the results you want, check out the causal actions. When you see a continual passing stream of people struggling in the raging river, go find out who is throwing them in. Who or what are the causal actions?

Spend your holidays doing nothing—nothing for work, everything for you. Spend your holidays reading, writing friends or writing your journal, exercising, hiking in uplifting venues, internet surfing for what interests you, all those activities that contribute to your personal growth and enjoyment. Make *Small Bites* a regular part of everyday, and a big part of your holidays.

An imperative subset of Responsibility is Discipline—doing *What* needs to be done *When* it needs to be done, especially when you don't feel like it.

One of my greatest privileges and pleasures has been coaching kids' sports, especially baseball. I love baseball, the thrill and challenge of the play. As a coach, I appreciate the value of practice and play in learning life lessons that transcend the athletic field: Discipline, Leadership, Teamwork, Commitment, Perseverance, and Resilience.

I coached youth baseball from kindergarten T-Ball to high school seniors. My favorite age is the Little Leaguers, aged 8 to 12. Kids of this age have begun to develop some skills, have some respect for authority, and are very coachable as they are still fascinated by life and their own possibilities.

On my teams we emphasized the responsibility and required discipline to practice 3 Magic Words:

- **Hustle** (use deliberate speed at all times)
- **Back-up** (support your appropriate teammate on every play)
- **N'Gup** (Never Give up! - regardless of score)

Responsible coaching, as well as parenting and management, improves skills and attitudes that develop personal confidence for improved execution. This requires the coach to teach how to preplan one's responsibilities on the field and at bat.

On Defense, our players were coached and challenged to analyze the current situation and proactively decide and audibly declare what they will do when the ball is hit. Who will they Back-up? Where will they throw the ball if it comes to them? When on Offense, prior to entering the batter's box, our players were coached to determine Where they would hit the ball, not If. They were preplanning their success. Ineffective attempts were practiced learning opportunities.

Our Team Rules were:

1. Always do your best in practice and games.
2. Look, listen, and learn when a coach is talking.
3. Always practice good sportsmanship.
4. Always respect your teammates and opponents.

I submit that these are pretty good lessons for life.

Duty

Always leave a place better than you found it.

- Dad

Always do the "most Important" first. Never let the trivial crowd out the important just because it's easier or feels good at the time.

- Dad

Where would you arrive – what could you achieve if every day you did just slightly better than the day before?

- Dad

I am here for a purpose and that purpose is to grow into a mountain, not to shrink to a grain of sand. Henceforth will I apply all my efforts to become the highest mountain of all, and I will strain my potential until it cries for mercy.

- Og Mandino

For everyone who has been given much, much will be demanded.

- Luke: 12:48

Exercising Responsibility creates Opportunities for Personal Growth, Contribution, and Joy.

- Dad

The willingness to accept responsibility for one's own life is the source from which self-respect springs.

– Joan Didion

Consequences…every action has them. Choose – Act wisely.

- Dad

Every day is a new beginning - a new "introduction" to your life. It's up to you what kind of "ending" you choose to write.

- Dad

Blaming others for your situation is like swimming with your hands behind your back. You might survive but what an inefficient way to get to where you want to go.

- Dad

Good vs. Good Enough

For most of my academic career I was pretty much an "A" student –not nearly the smartest, but I had learned to coast comfortably through school.

I got 88% on my first exam in Air Force Undergraduate Pilot training. This was the 5th lowest in a class of 90 student pilots. It became immediately apparent that "good" wasn't "good enough". It became even more clear that as a pilot there would be times when "what was learned" and "what was not" would make the difference between a successful mission—or not—even between life and death.

I adapted quickly.

Forgiveness is a process. Like "brushing your teeth" – it should be a continuous habit and expression of self-caring.

- Dad

It is better to light a candle than curse the darkness.

- Anonymous

You cannot escape the responsibility of tomorrow by evading it today.

- Abraham Lincoln

No one limits your growth but you. If you want to earn more, learn more. That means you'll work harder for a while; that means you'll work longer for a while. But you'll be paid for your extra effort with enhanced earnings down the road.

- Tom Hopkins

I am not bound to win, but I am bound to be true. I am not bound to succeed, but I am bound to live up to what light I have.

- Abraham Lincoln

It doesn't matter how strong your opinions are. If you don't use your power for positive change, you are, indeed, part of the problem.

- Coretta Scott King

You must constantly ask yourself these questions:
Who am I around?
What are they doing to me?
What have they got me reading?
What have they got me saying?
Where do they have me going?
What do they have me thinking?
And most important, what do they have me becoming?

Then ask yourself the big question: Is that okay?

- Jim Rohn

Example is not the main thing in influencing others. It is the only thing.

- Albert Schweitzer

As we express our gratitude, we must never forget that the highest appreciation is not to utter words, but to live by them.

- John Fitzgerald Kennedy

If it's your job to eat a frog, it's best to do it first thing in the morning. And If it's your job to eat two frogs, it's best to eat the biggest one first.

- Mark Twain

The game of life is the game of boomerangs. Our thoughts, deeds and words return to us sooner or later with astounding accuracy.

- Florence Scovel Shinn

3 A's?

How much more productive would you be if you intentionally turned every "complaint" into potentially resolving action?

- Dad

We are made wise not by the recollection of our past, but by the responsibility for our future.

- George Bernard Shaw

Nature gives you the face you have at twenty, it is up to you to merit the face you have at fifty.

- Coco Chanel

Let everyone sweep in front of his own door, and the whole world will be clean.

- Johann Wolfgang von Goethe

Acceptance of what has happened is the first step to overcoming the consequence of any misfortune.

- William James

Things turn out best for the people who make the best out of the way things turn out.

- Art Linkletter

Indecision and Inactivity are choices. So are Gratitude and Joy.

- Dad

Human progress is neither automatic nor inevitable. No social advance rolls in on the wheels of inevitability. Every step requires sacrifice, suffering, and struggle, the tireless exertions and passionate concern of dedicated individuals.

- Martin Luther King, Jr.

Young souls learn to accept responsibility for their actions. Mature souls learn to accept responsibility for their thoughts. And old souls learn to accept responsibility for their happiness.

- Anonymous

He who has a strong enough WHY can bear almost any HOW.

- Nietzsche

The fight is won or lost far away from witnesses - behind the lines, in the gym, and out there on the road, long before I dance under those lights.

- Muhammad Ali

Four short words sum up what has lifted most successful individuals above the crowd: a little bit more. They did all that was expected of them and a little bit more.

- A. Lou Vickery

Discipline is the bridge between goals and accomplishment.

- Jim Rohn

3 A's?

Self-discipline is when your conscience tells you to do something and you don't talk back.

- W.K. Hope

Self-respect is the root of discipline; the sense of dignity grows with the ability to say no to oneself.

- Abraham Lincoln

The most practical, beautiful, workable philosophy won't work- if you won't.

- Zig Ziglar

Life is not a "dress rehearsal".

- Vic Johnson

You can pay now and play later, or you can play now and pay later.

- John C. Maxwell

The thorns which I have reaped are of the tree I planted.

- George Gordon Noel

Be like a postage stamp – stick to it until you get there.

- Bob Proctor

Blame no one.
Expect nothing.
Do something.

- Bill Parcell

Continuous effort - not strength or intelligence - is the key to unlocking our potential.

- Sir Winston Churchill

Every day I get up and look at the Forbes list of the richest people in America. If I'm not on it, I go back to work.

- Robert Orben

There is no chance, no destiny, no fate that can circumvent or hinder or control the firm resolve of a determined soul.

- Ella Wheeler Wilcox

Obstacles cannot crush me. Every obstacle yields to stern resolve. He who is fixed to a star does not change his mind.

- Leonardo da Vinci

Don't be afraid if things seem difficult in the beginning. That's only the initial impression. The important thing is not to retreat; you have to master yourself.

- Olga Korbut

3 A's?

Our greatest weakness lies in giving up. The most certain way to succeed is always to try just one more time.

- Thomas Edison

We should every night call ourselves into account:
- What infirmity have I mastered today?
- What passions opposed?
- What temptation resisted?
- What virtue acquired?

- Marcus Annaeus Seneca

Winning isn't everything – the preparation and intention to Win/ Win is.

- Dad

The will to succeed is important, but what's more important is the will to prepare.

- Bobby Knight

The price of excellence is discipline.
The cost of mediocrity is disappointment.

- William Arthur Ward

All labor that uplifts humanity has dignity and importance.

Dr. Martin Luther King Jr.

What man is a man who does not make the world better?

- Anonymous

Unless someone like you cares a whole awful lot, nothing is going to get better. It's not.

- Uncle Lorax from Dr. Seuss

Notes

Record some of your own insights and decisions here

To get something you never had
you must do what you have never done.

- Anonymous

Every day do something that will inch you closer to a better to-
morrow.

- Doug Firebaugh

Chapter VIII

ACTION
(After-Burners)

There are only two mistakes one can make along the road to truth; not going all the way, and not starting.
- *Gautama Buddha*

People of accomplishment rarely sit back and let things happen to them. They went out and happened to things.
- *Elinore Regina Ward*

Like Robert Frost's Two roads diverged into a wood… two streams of thought diverge into different actions leading to different outcomes. When outcomes don't match hopes we can wallow remorsefully in the "woulda, shoulda, coulda" (WSC) of unmet expectations, cloaking ourselves in de-energizing disappointment or we can courageously don the armor of responsible action, acknowledging that no one other than self is at the controls and everyday allows us to reshape the WSC.

Jose Silva, the founder of the Silva Method, recommended the personal affirmation, "Everyday, in every way, you are getting better and better and better." My experience is that the affirmation's power is released only when one acts, as getting better is dependent on something changing and positive change only occurs when we are in motion.

Allow these *Small Bites* to be more than empty calories, reflect on them in a way that they become energizing vitamin boosters for taking action.

Brian Tracy, a personal growth coach, advises that,

All of life is a series of choices and decisions, actions and distinctions. The vital questions are, What distinctions and what actions are you making today?

3 A's?

The Bible teaches the law of sowing and reaping. It does not teach the law of reaping and sowing.

Time spent waiting that is used for refreshment or patiently analyzing and strategizing is useful. All other waiting is unproductive stalling. A Chinese proverb counsels that,

> *The best time to plant a tree was 20 years ago. The second best time is now.*

The poet, Dante Gabriel Rossetti wrote,

> *Look into my face, my name is "Might-have-been"; I am also called "No-more", "Too-late", "Farewell". Procrastination is a disease. An effective action is to procrastinate the procrastination.*

When you are a wise and responsible person you don't just choose those things that feel good or that you want to do. You choose those that have an impact on your greater well-being and that of your family and community.

If communication is the response you get, your life experience is the response you give.

To optimize our life experience we need to work to create a vision that inspires us and catapults us into action. From the movie *Shawshank Redemption*, we learned that,

> *You either get busy living, or you get busy dying.*

After Burners

Life is what you make it. Always was – always will be.
                                                                    - Grandma Moses

Footprints on the sands of time are not made by sitting down.
                                                                    - Anonymous

It is Not the Critic That Counts

It is not the critic that counts; not the man who points out how the strong man stumbles, or where the doer of deeds could have done better. The credit belongs to the man who is actually in the arena, whose face is marred by dust and sweat and blood; who strives valiantly; who errs, and comes short again and again, because there is no effort without error and shortcoming; who knows the great enthusiasms, the great devotions; who spends himself in a worthy cause; who at best knows in the end the triumph of high achievement. And at worst, if he fails, at least fails while daring greatly, so that his place shall never be with those cold and timid souls who know neither victory nor defeat.

- President Theodore Roosevelt, Paris 1910

Heroes are honored for positive results; results flow from continually trying - learning what doesn't work, and trying something new. Trying is the first step in every achievement.
                                                                    - Dad

Things only happen in a moment of decision.
                                                                    - Anonymous

Nothing splendid has ever been achieved except by those who felt something inside them was superior to circumstances.

- Bruce Barton

Knowledge may give weight, but accomplishments give luster, and many more people see than weigh.

- Philip Donner Stanhope

Failing to prepare is preparing to fail.

- Coach John Wooden

Remember there is nothing that you can't make better if you apply energy to imagination.

- Dad

The best way to predict the future is to create it.

- Peter F. Drucker

The way to do things is to begin.

- Albert Einstein

You don't have to be great to get started, but you have to get started to be great.

- Les Brown

Things do not happen. Things are made to happen.
                                            - John F. Kennedy

It is easier to change direction once in motion.
                                            - Anonymous

Wishing is not doing.
                                            - Dad

Great ideas don't interrupt you. You've got to pursue them.
                                            - Anthony Robbins

Make it count. If not "now", "when"? Stacked-up "whens" don't become "Wins".
                                            - Dad

Until One is Committed

Until one is committed, there is hesitancy,
the chance to draw back, always ineffectiveness.

Concerning all acts of initiative (and creation),
there is one elementary truth,
the ignorance of which kills countless ideas and splendid plans:
that the moment one definitely commits oneself,
then providence moves too.

A whole stream of events issues from the decision,
raising in one's favor all manner of unforeseen incidents,
meetings and material assistance,
which no man could have dreamt would have come his way.

I learned a deep respect for one of Goethe's couplets:
Whatever you can do or dream you can, begin it.
Boldness has genius, power and magic in it!

- William Huchison Murray

There is no next time. It's now or never.

- Anonymous

A work well begun is half-ended.

- Plato

When you have exhausted all possibilities; remember this: you haven't.

- Thomas Edison

Take action to ensure that Not Now's do not become Never Will's.
- Dad

The only time you run out of chances is when you stop taking them.
- Michael Josephson

The dog that trots about finds a bone.
- Golda Meir

There are only two mistakes one can make along the road to truth; not going all the way, and not starting.
- Gautama Buddha

Two Lines
1) Those who take action today: Healthy, Wealthy, & Wise
2) Those who "put-off" until tomorrow: Feeble, Procrastinators, Whiners
We always have a choice in which Line to stand.
- Dad

Intention is not enough. Anger at injustice unmatched with corrective action is cancerous. Be the change you wish to see.
- Dad

Small deeds done are better than great deeds planned.
- Peter Marshall

3 A's?   99

The journey of a thousand leagues begins with the first step.

- Confucius

How do you eat an elephant?
One bite at a time.

- Anonymous

The person who removes a mountain begins by carrying away small stones.

- Chinese Proverb

How wonderful it is that nobody need wait a single moment before starting to improve the world

- Anne Frank

Act now. Reflect later. Life is an action movie.

- Dad

Opportunity does not knock, it presents itself when you beat down the door.

- Kyle Chandler

I do not believe in a fate that falls on men however they act; but I do believe in a fate that falls on them unless they act.

- Gautama Buddha

3 A's?

Waiting for Success is like standing at the top of the slope and thinking that you are skiing. You must launch yourself.

- Dad

You can't expect to hit the jackpot if you don't put a few nickels in the machine.

- Flip Wilson

There comes a moment when you have to stop revving up the car and shove it into gear.

– David Mahoney

Moving forward on one's dreams is like basketball. You don't make every shot – but you miss every one you don't take.

- Dad

Translating insights and strong feelings into "Intention" is the Key. Taking "Action" is the Answer.

- Dad

Action is a great restorer and builder of confidence.
Inaction is not only the result, but the cause, of fear.
Perhaps the action you take will be successful;
Perhaps different action or adjustments will have to follow.
But any action is better than no action at all.

- Norman Vincent Peale

Nearly everything you do is of no importance, but it is important that you do it.

- Mohandas Gandhi

Now is the Beginning of the Next. Take Stock. Act. Serve Others.

- Dad

Keep striving. Complacency is a disease.

- Dad

Wisdom is knowing what to do next; virtue is doing it.

- David Starr Jordan

When taking stock, if you are not feeling or being what you want – change direction.

- Dad

As Aristotle said, "We are what we do repeatedly." Therefore let your "doing" guide and be guided-by your goals.

- Dad

Keep on going, and the chances are that you will stumble on something, perhaps when you are least expecting it. I never heard of anyone ever stumbling on something sitting down.

- Charles F. Kettering

3 A's?

Don't wait. The time will never be just right.

- Napoleon Hill

Success doesn't come to you, you go to it.

- Marva Collins

I hated every minute of training, but I said, Don't quit. Suffer now and live the rest of your life as a champion.

- Muhammad Ali

An ounce of practice is worth more than tons of preaching.

- Mohandas Gandhi

Some people talk change.
Others cause change.

- Hubert Humphrey

My life is my message.
How am I going to live today in order to create the tomorrow I'm committed to?

- Anthony Robbins

If you are going through hell, keep going.

- Winston Churchill

3 A's?

Not knowing when the dawn will come, I open every door.
- Emily Dickinson

God gives us the nuts – but He does not crack them.
- Old Proverb

Who seeks shall find.
- Sophocles

When you can't change the direction of the wind—adjust your sails.
- H. Jackson Brown

Doubt, of whatever kind, can be ended by action alone.
- Thomas Carlyle

Better to do something imperfectly than to do nothing flawlessly.
- Robert H. Schuler

Thought-Leaders must be Doing-Leaders.
- Dad

The highways of life are full of flat squirrels who couldn't make up their minds.
- Anonymous

3 A's?

Fix your eyes forward on what you can do, not back on what you cannot change.

- Tom Clancy

To Do is to Be.

- Socrates

To Be is to Do.

- Jean Paul Sartre

One of the virtues of the very young is that you don't let facts get in the way of your imagination.

- Sam Levinson

Time has come today
Can't put it off another day
I don't care what others say
They say we don't listen anyway
Time has come today

Now the time has come
There are things to realize
Time has come today

- The Chambers Brothers
from song **Time Has Come Today**

What you do today can improve all your tomorrows.

- Ralph Marston

The winds of grace are always blowing for it is you that must raise your sails.

- Rabindranath Tagore

Do what you can, with what you have, where you are.

- Theodore Roosevelt

Doing nothing is doing something. Some of the worst decisions are the ones that were never made.

- Michael Josephson

Right actions for the future are the best apologies for wrong ones in the past.

- Tyron Edwards

Fate laughs at probabilities.

- E.G. Bulwer-Lytton

An idea not coupled with action will never get any bigger than the brain cell it occupied.

- Arnold Glasgow

Thunder is good, thunder is impressive; but it is lightning that does the work.

- Mark Twain

3 A's?

Your life does not get better by chance, it gets better by change.
                                                          - Jim Rohn

Conditions are never just right. People who delay action, until all factors are favorable, are the kind who do nothing.
                                                    - William Feather

Most people "know what to do". The problem is that they "don't do what they know."
                                                   - Anthony Robbins

Don't ask what the world needs. Ask what makes you come alive, and go do it. Because what the world needs is people who have come alive.
                                                  - Howard Thurman

Action expresses priorities.
                                                 - Mohandas Gandhi

Hard work spotlights the character of people: Some turn up their sleeves, some turn up their noses, and some don't turn up at all.
                                                       - Sam Ewing

Time has no conscience... it doesn't judge...it only mirrors... what you have put into your time...it mirrors back as your life.
                                                   - Doug Firebaugh

3 A's?

Circumstances do not make the man, they reveal him.

- James Allen

There are some people who live in a dream world, and there are some who face reality; and then there are those who turn one into the other.

- Douglas H. Everett

The world is but a canvas to our imaginations.

- Henry David Thoreau

The difference between great people and everyone else is that great people create their lives actively, while everyone else is created by their lives, passively waiting to see where life takes them next. The difference between the two is the difference between living fully and just existing.

- Michael E. Gerber

You are not defined by "what you have". "What you are" is a projection of "what you do". Be responsible to make "what you do" is complementary to "what you value".

- Dad

The artist is nothing without the gift, but the gift is nothing without work.

- Emile Zola

3 A's?

If you hear a voice within you say "you cannot paint," then by all means paint, and that voice will be silenced.

- Vincent Van Gogh

Life happens at the level of events, not of words. Trust movement.

- Michael Josephson

Instead of worrying about what people say of you, why not spend time trying to accomplish something they will admire.

- Dale Carnegie

Make sure that your actions and behaviors live up to and reflect the words and ideas, promises and commitments that come out of your mouth.

- Steve Farber

Do not wait for leaders. Do it alone, person to person.

- Mother Theresa

The meeting of preparation with opportunity generates the off-spring we call luck.

- Anthony Robbins

We are all faced with a series of great opportunities brilliantly disguised as impossible situations.

- Charles R. Swindoll

3 A's?

To Speak or not to Speak:
If it is not truthful and not helpful don't say it.
If it is truthful and not helpful don't say it.
If it is not truthful and helpful don't say it
If it is both truthful and helpful ... Wait for the right time.
- Gautama Buddha

Don't tell me how hard you work. Tell me how much you get done.
- James Ling

Many men may doubt what you say, but they will believe what you do.
- Lewis Cass

Many persons invest heavily of their time and money in trainings and materials to gain knowledge only to have the "learning" gather dust on the shelves of inactivity. To Know is to Do.
- Dad

To know what is right and not do it is the worst cowardice.
- Confucius

Yesterday is a dream. Tomorrow is a vision. But today, well lived, makes every yesterday a dream of happiness and every tomorrow a vision of hope.
- Anonymous

3 A's?

Always finish strong! Weak beginnings can sometimes be overcome. Poor endings usually promote regrets and lost opportunities.

- Dad

Man is born to live and not to prepare to live.

- Boris Pasternak

It is better to travel well than to arrive.

- Gautama Buddha

Five birds are sitting on a telephone wire. Two of them decide to fly South. How many are left? Three, you say? No, it's five. You see, deciding to fly South is not the same as doing it. Good intentions are not enough. It's action that really matters.

- Michael Josephson

Notes
Record some of your own insights and decisions here

When you face your fear,
most of the time you will discover
that it was not really such a big threat after all.
We all need some form of deeply rooted,
powerful motivation
—it empowers us to overcome obstacles
so we can live our dreams.

- Les Brown

Chapter IX

COURAGE
(Tailwind)

Courage is an essential ingredient in Success and personal development. The absence of courage results in many missed opportunities and too many painful ones. Although courage can be learned, it is not learned from another. It is something you discover from within yourself. Discovering for oneself what is needed or wanted is more important than the potential feeling of failure.

Courage refrains from taking foolish risks with safety or resources. Courage is not jumping without looking. A pilot's adage is,

There are old pilots and there are bold pilots but there are no old bold pilots.

Real boldness and courage require careful analysis of the situation, reviewing your options, and selecting those that serve you best. Goethe preached,

(real) Boldness has Genius, Power, and Magic in it.

Courage often requires corralling one's inner demons and initially pretending that you are courageous. Like any skill, courage gets better with practice. Your courage muscles get pumped up by exercising them.

Courage is an attitude. Select your attitudes and relationships that serve you best. Pick those that you hang with carefully. It has be said that,

If you always live with those that are lame, you yourself will learn to limp. Conversely, if you are soaring with the eagles you probably won't learn to quack.

Tailwind

Fear has its use but cowardice has none.

- Mohandas Gandhi

Courage and Success are not fostered from "Winning" – they are nurtured through the willful acts of "showing-up" and playing with passion.

- Dad

Importantly, in every game, including the "Game of Life", you've got to let your mistakes GO. You've got to keep your head up and try, try again… and again…and again.

- Dad

Rise and Rise again. Until Lambs become Lions.

- Sir Walter Longstride
*from **The Tales of Robin Hood***

The greatest glory in living lies not in never falling, but in rising every time we fall.

- Nelson Mandela

Courage is also doing what you don't feel like doing when it needs to be done.

- Dad

3 A's?

When you need Courage and you don't feel it – review your choices, their likely outcomes and then "act as if" you were appropriately Courageous. It's your best option.

- Dad

Courage is not something you get – it is something you give – to yourself. It comes from within and is expressed through "right action".

- Dad

Courage is like muscles and push-ups, the more you practice, the more they grow.

- Dad

When the outcome is in doubt, Courage is a "faith-based product of self-resourcefulness" trumping "fear of failure".

- Dad

Courage is an expression of "self-trust" overcoming "self-doubt".

- Dad

It's hard to beat a person who never gives up.

- Babe Ruth

Never let the fear of striking out get in your way.

- Babe Ruth

3 A's?   117

Within you, right now, is the power to do things you never dreamed possible. This power becomes available to you just as soon as you can change your beliefs.

- Dr. Maxwell Maltz

It's not how hard you can "hit". It's how hard you can "get hit" and keep pressing forward.

- Rocky Balboa
from the film Rocky IV

Success is failure turned inside out -
The silver tint of the clouds of doubt,
And you never can tell how close you are -
It may be near when it seems afar;
So stick to the fight when you're hardest hit -
It's when things seem worst that you mustn't quit.

- Edgar A. Guest

First they ignore you.
Then they laugh at you.
Then they fight you.
Then you win.

- Mahatma Gandhi

Courage is being scared to death— and saddling up anyway.
- John Wayne

Courage is not the absence of fear, but rather the judgment that something else is more important than fear.

- Ambrose Redmoon

Courage is resistance to fear, mastery of fear, not absence of fear.
- Mark Twain

He who is not courageous enough to take risks will accomplish nothing in life.

- Muhammad Ali

Courage is not limited to the battlefield. The real tests of courage are much quieter. They are the inner tests, like enduring pain when the room is empty or standing alone.

- Charles Swindall

I have not ceased being fearful, but I have ceased to let fear control me.

- Erica Jong

Fear cannot be without hope nor hope without fear.
- Baruch Spinoza

Although Courage lives by risk, including the risk of failure, it also is the seed of expanded Insight, Growth, and Opportunity.
- Dad

When you are faced with something that gives you fear, realize that fear is of man's mind, not God's mind.

- Sheradon Bryce

If you want to take the island you have to burn the boats.

- Anonymous

Necessity is the mother of taking chances.

- Mark Twain

Heroes are just people who continue to move forward when others are stuck in "complaint-itis".

- Dad

Fear does not have any special power unless you empower it by submitting to it.

- Les Brown

Blindfolded fear does not lead to an Awakening. Questioning with Boldness does.

- Thomas Jefferson

Throughout the centuries there were men who took first steps, down new roads, armed with nothing but their own vision.

- Ayn Rand

3 A's?

Courage is what it takes to stand up and speak;
Courage is also what it takes to sit down and listen.
- Winston Churchill

The future does not belong to the feint-hearted. It belongs to the brave.
- President Ronald Reagan

Whatever course you decide upon, there is always someone to tell you that you are wrong. There are always difficulties arising which tempt you to believe that your critics are right. To map out a course of action and follow it to an end requires...courage.
- Ralph Waldo Emerson

It's always too early to quit.
- Norman Vincent Peale

Courage is the ladder on which all the other virtues mount.
- Clare Booth Luce

Never grow a wishbone where your backbone ought to be.
- Clementine Paddleford

The fishermen know that the sea is dangerous and the storm terrible, but they have never found these dangers sufficient reasons for remaining ashore.
- Vincent Van Gogh

Be determined to handle any challenge in a way that will make you grow.

- Les Brown

Courage doesn't always roar.   Sometimes courage is the little voice at the end of the day that says I'll try again tomorrow.

- Mary Anne Radmacher

The trouble is, if you don't risk anything, you risk even more.

- Erica Jong

Any coward can fight a battle when he's sure of winning, but give me the man who has pluck to fight when he's sure of losing.

- George Eliot

Success is not final, failure is not fatal: it is the courage to continue that counts.

- Sir Winston Churchill

Courage is not always enough to assure victory, but it demonstration while confronting challenges and pursuing victory brings its own rewards not the least of which is knowledge that fear did not and will not keep you from the battle.

- Michael Josephson

3 A's?

You gain strength, courage, and confidence by every experience in which you really stop to look fear in the face. You are able to say to yourself, "I have lived through this horror. I can take the next thing that comes along." You must do the thing that you cannot do.

- Eleanor Roosevelt

There is within you, waiting to be called, a great source of power called courage. Call its name and it will give you the strength to overcome fear and uncertainty and the heart to continue with bold confidence despite the pain of disappointment and even tragedy.

- Michael Josephson

It Takes Courage

It takes strength to be firm,
It takes courage to be gentle.

It takes strength to conquer,
It takes courage to surrender.

It takes strength to be certain,
It takes courage to have doubt.

It takes strength to fit in,
It takes courage to stand out.

It takes strength to feel a friend's pain,
It takes courage to feel your own pain.

It takes strength to endure abuse,
It takes courage to stop it.

It takes strength to stand alone,
It takes courage to lean on another.

It takes strength to love,
It takes courage to be loved.

It takes strength to survive,
It takes courage to live.

- David L. Griffin

3 A's?

Notes

Record some of your own insights and decisions here

The

best

way

out

is

always

through.

- Robert Frost

Chapter X

ADVERSITY
(Turbulence - Emergency Procedures)

When an in-flight mechanical failure occurs a pilot spends his focus blaming the plane at great peril.

- Dad

I don't measure a man's success by how high he climbs but how high he bounces when he hits bottom.

- General George S. Patton

Handling adversity or unexpected turbulence requires a sharp focus on what should be done first. As mentioned in the chapter on Attitude, pilots are trained to memorize critical Emergency Procedures for nearly all conceived emergencies. These must be conducted in specific order. The procedures are continually practiced until the pilot becomes fully functionally competent in proceeding through the memorized checklist.

Outside the cockpit, adversities in life are usually a confluence or accumulation of events. Rarely are there a set of exactly appropriate procedures that can be immediately applied to correct the situation. However, there are actions to take to insure greater success in transiting through the turbulence.

The right Attitude supplemented with appropriate Courage is more likely to lead to the right Actions. Anthony Robbins advises that it is vital to see things as they are, not worse than they are and act to change things to be as you want them to be.

My high school football coach drilled the principle into our head that, "When you are within the 10 yard line, don't drop the damn ball." I have worked to apply this principle to my businesses and my relationships.

Formerly, I had perceived this warning as to not lose focus or commitment when you were near your goal. Although I recognize this wise caution, my life experience has taught me that the greatest risk is to lose focus or commitment when you are on your heels, nearly under water, or when your goals and success seem quite distant.

I have found these times most crucial for personal achievement. For a leader, the recognition, energy, and activity required for effectively coping and moving forward during times of crisis are more important than any other time. It is within the environment of chaos that leadership is exposed. It is the most difficult time to marshal personal and team resources. Crises are the true test of personal effectiveness and leadership. As a wise person wrote,

It is easy enough to be pleasant,
When life flows by like a song,
But the man worth while
Is one who will smile,
When everything goes dead wrong.

- Ella Wheeler Wilcox

The old saying, "Easier said than done", is only relevant when we are stuck in inertia spending more time complaining than acting. Michael Josephson advises,

When you are in a hole, stop digging.

Effective personal and organizational leadership must be uplifting, not "downbeating". It must be creative, visionary, and appropriately risk-taking.

During crises, risk must be managed. But first, it must be understood. Bob Lutz, a guru at General Motors, advises that in times of crisis a measure of "productive paranoia" is useful. Fanatic discipline to manage risk must be empirical in focus, a rigorous assessment of the facts, and actions to root out what actually works and what does not.

Effective leadership must be disciplined to constantly focus on which attitudes correlate to successful action and which actions correlate to successful results. Disciplined focus and activity lead to increased resilience and faith. As Steve Jobs said,

Sometimes life is going to hit you in the face with a brick. Don't lose faith.

Faith is not relying on the anticipation of good luck. Good luck cannot be the foundation for success. Faith in self is the well from which personal resourcefulness can flow. Faith in self is an essential ingredient to overcome threats to survival, be they personal or organizational.

Faith provides the stimulus to stay in motion. The key is to do what is known to work. For the individual, it is exercise, nutrition, journaling, networking, working a plan. For the leader, it is collaborating, inspiring, guiding, and leading from the front. Many of the *Small Bites* emphasize these principles, especially in the chapters on Courage, Success, and Action.

Every football running back can attest that it is easier to change direction when in motion. Remember that every unexpected adversity creates possibilities for a different experience. There are no failures in life, only lessons. Wisdom is earned when you embrace the lessons in every failure. These are often hidden and often with unanticipated opportunities.

Like the undaunted young man excited by the pile of horse manure claiming, "There must be a pony around here someplace!" our challenge is always to look for the pony, the opportunity, while handling the turbulence. Many *Small Bites* speak to this wisdom.

Turbulence - Emergency Procedures

Make a commitment that tragedies and disappointments become a source of increased Patience, Strength, & Wisdom.

- Dad

If you are going through hell, keep going.

- Winston Churchill

In skating over thin ice, our safety is in our speed.

- Ralph Waldo Emerson

A crisis is a terrible thing to waste.

- Anonymous

God sometimes does try to the uttermost those whom he wishes to bless.

- Mohandas Gandhi

A certain amount of opposition is a great help to a man. Kites rise against, not with the wind.

- John Neal

3 A's?

Mishaps are like knives that either cut us or serve us as we grasp them by the blade or the handle.

- James Russell Lowell

The biggest catastrophe of experiencing extreme stress, ego-wrenching embarrassment, or even near-death may be that we don't learn from it.

- Dad

All failure is temporary. Temporary failure is never an excuse for quitting.

- Dad

If you want to enjoy the rainbow, be prepared to endure the storm.
- Warren Wendel Wieisbe

Adversity introduces a man to himself.

- Anonymous

Do not rely completely on any other human being, however dear. We meet all life's greatest tests alone.
- Agnes Campbell MacPhail

If...

IF you can keep your head when all about you
Are losing theirs and blaming it on you,

If you can trust yourself when all men doubt you,
But make allowance for their doubting too;

If you can wait and not be tired by waiting,
Or being lied about, don't deal in lies,

Or being hated, don't give way to hating,
And yet don't look too good, nor talk too wise:

If you can dream - and not make dreams your master;
If you can think - and not make thoughts your aim;

If you can meet with Triumph and Disaster
And treat those two impostors just the same;

If you can bear to hear the truth you've spoken
Twisted by knaves to make a trap for fools,

Or watch the things you gave your life to, broken,
And stoop and build 'em up with worn-out tools:

If you can make one heap of all your winnings
And risk it on one turn of pitch-and-toss,

And lose, and start again at your beginnings
And never breathe a word about your loss;

If you can force your heart and nerve and sinew
To serve your turn long after they are gone,

And so hold on when there is nothing in you
Except the Will which says to them: "Hold on!"

3 A's?

If you can talk with crowds and keep your virtue,
"Or walk with Kings, nor lose the common touch,

if neither foes nor loving friends can hurt you,
If all men count with you, but none too much;

If you can fill the unforgiving minute
With sixty seconds' worth of distance run,

Yours is the Earth and everything that's in it,
And—which is more—you'll be a Man, my son!

- Rudyard Kipling

3 A's?

Problems are not stop signs, they are guidelines.

- Robert Schuller

Turn your wounds into wisdom.

- Oprah Winfrey

Negotiating unwanted turbulence is an opportunity to sharpen one's skills.

- Dad

Drag your thoughts away from your troubles... by the ears, by the heels, or any other way you can manage it.

- Mark Twain

You never will be the person you can be if pressure, tension and discipline are taken out of your life.

- James G. Bilkey

Only a man who knows what it is like to be defeated can reach down to the bottom of his soul and come up with the extra ounce of power it takes to win when the match is even.

- Muhammad Ali

3 A's?

Stuck in a Box???

Feeling "Closed-in"?
No Progress?
Can't Escape?

Personal story: Air Force POW/Survival Training

As an U.S. Air Force pilot in the early '70's, I underwent POW/Survival training. The training was to teach skills that would allow you to survive in the wilderness with no food, tools, or companions, using only your wits and the resources available in jungle or forest habitat. The training was very rigorous and demanding.

The training was also designed to prepare you for the extreme duress of being a Prisoner of War (POW).

One process used to simulate the isolation and torture that would likely be experienced as a POW was, after much physical and mental harassment, to lock you into "pitch black" box about the size of a small washing machine. This was extremely uncomfortable and nearly mentally unbearable.

The time spent "in the box", although usually less than an hour each time, seemed to last forever, kind of like in life, when you are experiencing a rut, depression, or severe problem with no solution in sight.

The box experience was transforming. For some, it was so horrific that they failed the test and did not complete the training. I even heard comments like, "If being a POW is anything like the training, I'll never let them take me alive!" For others, the box experience was motivational. Motivating from the point of view that even with the nearly unbearable anguish, we could "come through", complete the test, and move forward.

The box became a symbol of our inner strength and commitment to do whatever is necessary to survive, to succeed, to care for ourselves, our family, our country. I trust that this was the real intention of the learning exercises.

Many of us who completed the test shared reflections that regardless of the physical and mental suffering we were sustained by knowing that it was a simulation; that the Air Force had just spent a million dollars training us as pilots, and the faith that they were really on our side.

This comforting and sustaining awareness was crucial to survival. And so it is with all of our life experiences. What if you lived your life believing that the Universe is really on your side?

It is my firm belief that we were not given life for no reason. Not yet knowing the reason is not justification for not embracing the nurture of a sustaining Universe. Treading in the comfort of a purposeful and nurturing Universe gives us strength to move through life's challenges, and it inspires and stimulates us to move toward greater insight, wisdom, well-being, and contribution.

The magic of life is that these are different for everyone and we get to play in a world of unlimited diversity, beauty, privilege, and opportunity. And it always starts from where we are— now!

So what box are you in? Where do you want to go armed with the knowledge and faith that the Universe will support?

Remember, even with such support, it's You in the box and it's You who must do the doing to move through and toward your challenges and contributions.

So our next questions should be, What do I want to do? and What will I do to get there?

It is my personal belief that the necessary expression of appreciation for the Universe's support is Action and Service for the benefit of others.

> *Behind me is infinite power.*
> *Before me is endless possibility.*
> *Around me is boundless opportunity.*
> *Why should I fear?*
>
> - *Stella Stuart*

Invictus

Out of the night that covers me,
Black as the pit from pole to pole,
I thank whatever gods may be
For my unconquerable soul.

In the fell clutch of circumstance
I have not winced nor cried aloud.
Under the bludgeonings of chance
My head is bloody, but unbowed.

Beyond this place of wrath and tears
Looms but the Horror of the shade,
And yet the menace of the years
Finds, and shall find, me unafraid.

It matters not how strait the gate,
How charged with punishments the scroll,
I am the master of my fate:
I am the captain of my soul.

- William Ernest Henley

Forget past mistakes. Forget failures. Forget about everything
except what you're going to do now—and do it.
- William Durant

Life is often full of pain and trouble
Only losers let these burst their bubble.

- Anonymous

3 A's?

Worrying is like a rocking chair: it gives you something to do, but it doesn't get you anywhere.

- Anonymous

Importantly, in every game, including the "Game of Life", you've got to let your mistakes GO. You've got to keep your head up and try, try again… and again…and again.

- Dad

No man ever became great or good except through many and great mistakes.

- William E. Gladstone

No one rises above who he or she has been without first having fallen down. The best time - in fact, the only time - to make a real change in your life is in the moment of seeing the need for it. He who hesitates always gets lost in the hundred reasons why tomorrow is a better day to get started.

- Guy Finley

No steam or gas ever drives anything until it is confined.
No Niagara is ever turned into light and power until it is tunneled.
No life ever grows until it is focused, dedicated and disciplined.

- Harry Emerson Fosdick

When an in-flight mechanical failure occurs a pilot spends his focus blaming the plane at great peril.

- Dad

3 A's?

It is not falling into the water, but lying in it, that drowns.

- Anonymous

Even if you fall on your face, you're still moving forward.

- Victor Kiam

Pain is inevitable but suffering is optional.

- Anonymous

Flowers grow out of darker moments.

- Corita Kent

The heart, like the grape, is prone to delivering its harvest in the same moment that it is about to be crushed.

- Roger Houseden

Storms make Oaks take deeper roots.

- George Herbert

The ultimate measure of a man is not where he stands in moments of comfort and convenience, but where he stands at times of challenge and controversy.

- Martin Luther King, Jr.

3 A's?

It takes a real storm in the average person's life to make him realize how much worrying he has done over the squalls.
                                    - Anonymous

The harder the conflict, the more glorious the triumph.
                                    - Thomas Paine

Failure is only the opportunity to begin again more intelligently.
                                    - Henry Ford

Never doubt that your focused will is enough to overcome disappointments, frustrations, and even great tragedies.
                                    - Michael Josephson

People may fail many times, but they become failures only when they begin to blame someone else. Experience is determined by yourself -- not the circumstances of your life.
                                    - Gita Bellin

It isn't the mountains ahead to climb that wear you out; it's the pebble in your shoe.
                                    - Muhammad Ali

Disappointments, defeat, despair are the tools God uses to show us the way.
                                    - Pablo Coelho

If you are lost, go faster; you won't be lost as long.

- Anonymous

All the adversity I've had in my life, all my troubles have strengthened me...you may not realize it when it happens, but a kick in the teeth may be the best thing in the world for you.

- Walt Disney

While in the air, if you have time to think about: girlfriend, golf, food, or whiskey, something bad is about to happen.

- Anonymous Pilot

Not everything that is faced can be changed. But nothing can be changed until it is faced.

- James Baldwin

It is easy enough to be pleasant,
  When life flows by like a song,
But the man worthwhile is one who will smile,
  When everything goes dead wrong.

- Ella Wheeler Wilcox

Don't taunt the alligator until after you've crossed the creek.

- Dan Rather

Winds of Fate

One ship drives east and another drives west
With the selfsame winds that blow.

'Tis the set of the sails,
And Not the gales,
That tell us the way to go.

Like the winds of the sea are the ways of fate;
As we voyage along through life,

'Tis the set of a soul
That decides its goal,
And not the calm or the strife.

- *Ella Wheeler Wilcox*

3 A's?

Notes
Record some of your own insights and decisions here

Chapter XI

LEADERSHIP & MANAGEMENT
(Formation Flying)

Vision without Action is a daydream.
Acton without Vision is a nightmare.

- *Japanese Proverb*

Leadership is a "can-do", "get-it-done",
"everyone-pull-together", "whatever-it- takes" attitude.

- *Orville Schell*

Giving homage to the thousands of books on management techniques, I still claim that Leadership and Management are more art than science, although techniques can be learned. Effective techniques must accommodate culture and environment. Measuring and monitoring what is actually occurring with management interventions must be ongoing. Timely decisiveness is crucial to effective management and leadership. We must learn to take advantage of current fortune and be alert not to relax or underinvest in developing future options.

Always have a back-up plan.
Always have an exit strategy.
Always have an alternative airfield.

Always start your Plan with 4W + H:
- What?
- Who?
- Where?
- Why?
- How?

Colin Powell advised that the probability of success for any endeavor requires obtaining 40 to 70 percent of the essential information and then "go with your gut".

A good friend, who is a very senior executive of Chevron, advises the following,

Good leaders are well grounded, introspective and humble. They never let power or ego blind them. Good leaders have passion and a bias for action. Leaders are not afraid to make mistakes but they are determined to learn from them. Responsible leaders don't accept the status quo and always work to change the outcome. These leaders see the innate potential in people and unlock it. Through inspiration and role-modeling, these leaders win the hearts and minds of everyone around them and get more from their people than humanly possible.

Management and Leadership must co-exist. Good observation skills coupled with people-skills are essential for effective Management / Leadership. The insights offered with these *Small Bites* recommend combing the guiding and providing of essential resources and support with nurture and caring for the development and the well-being of team members.

Successful Leadership / Management strategies and processes must emanate from the synergistic intersection where courage, action, and responsibility meet.

3 A's?

Six P's of Effective Leadership / Management

Proper Prior Planning Prevents Poor Performance.

My Operating Definition of Leadership:

Lead – to be out-in-front
Ship – a transport system

Therefore, for me, Leadership is a process that moves you forward, puts you out-in-front, that is synonymous with influence, authority, power, the ability to get things done. This process is vital for personal and organizational effectiveness.

Responsible leadership is taking charge, even if only of oneself, to move toward a better place.

These *Small Bites* have value and authority even if you are only a leader of one. It is the interaction of the initiatives of the responsible ones that will improve your life, and our world.

While researching principles for Leadership several concepts became apparent:

1. The wisdom and advice for improved life experience through personal resolve apply to effective Responsible Leadership
2. The corollary is also true: the principles for Responsible Leadership apply to strengthening personal resolve and enhancing an individual's life experience.

The principles of Responsible Leadership, the attributes, and the contributions are goals and actions that anyone can use in any situation.

Leadership is a privilege. An appreciative public showers effective responsible leaders with acknowledgment and social and financial benefits.

My selection of *Small Bites* represents my primary life-bias. My comments in introducing *Small Bites* were not originally intended to editorialize as the categories and selections speak for themselves. The chapter headings are themselves a recommended pathway. Yet, I concur with recent criticisms about the loss of focus on the important things driving social and personal progress.

Since the 1980's, in my opinion, too many of our brightest young people, those most likely harboring the promise of greatest social contributions, have chosen not to work in the fields related to STEMM (Science, Technology, Engineering, Math, and Medicine). Many instead have opted to work in the Wall Street linked industries where relatively less lasting social value is created or contributed. Many suggest that this imbalance of talent and power in the financial industries have exacerbated the dangers of debt-fuelled economic growth and spirally debt crises with the social ills of growing inequality and money influence on politics.

Some of the major societal growth drivers, which need our near-term attention and improvement are: public education, physical health and fitness, energy grids, land-based and digital infrastructures and accessibility. Although the Liberal Arts contribute great value in lifting the human spirit, the STEMM competencies are in short supply and are needed to address many of the major issues impacting our societies.

Formation Flying

Building on others' good ideas, with proper acknowledgment, is true flattery and a sign of wisdom.

- Dad

The challenge of leadership is to
-be Strong, but not rude;
-be Kind, but not weak;
-be Bold, but not a bully;
-be Thoughtful, but not lazy;
-be Humble, but not timid;
-be Proud but not arrogant;
-have Humor, but without folly.

- Jim Rohn

Surround yourself with persons who can do crucial tasks better than you.

- Dad

I not only use all the brains that I have, but all that I can borrow.
- Woodrow Wilson

Those who are lifting the world upward and onward are those who encourage more than criticize.

- Elizabeth Harrison

Fast Pants

Before a fighter pilot climbs into his aircraft he dons his *Fast Pants*. These pants (anti-G suit) fitted with air bladders automatically inflate when high G-forces are experienced. The inflated bladders prevent blood from pooling in the lower body and depriving the brain of oxygen-rich blood to help prevent loss of sight and consciousness.

I suggest that Responsible Leaders intentionally don virtual fast pants when they enter a crisis to help them see clearly, avoid tunnel vision, and remain conscious of what's needed, and what's not.

What's important, and what's not?

The first leg of my virtual fast pants requires me to answer the following questions:

1. Who should I collaborate with?
2. What are the 2 to 3 most important issues to resolve in this situation?
3. What are the most appropriate, timely, and available resources that apply to resolutions?

Pulling on the second leg I ask:

1. What are the action priorities?
2. What should I do Now?

My memory aid to remind me of these processes:

- Collaborate	C
- Issues	I
- Resources	R
- Priority	P
- Action	A

Collaboratively work *Issues* with *Resources Prioritized* for *Action*

3 A's?

Collaboration is the Key.
Acknowledgment is the Answer.

It's not from the known, but the unknown, that creativity and inventiveness are born. Synergy released through guided collaboration produces uncommon results. Leaders creating processes that encourage and reward collaboration more often achieve innovative and profitable solutions for the benefit of all concerned.

A *peloton* is the main group of riders in a cycling road race. The group saves energy by riding close together, drafting and slipstreaming with each other; there's a tactical element near the end as the strongest riders break from the pack to win, often with support from team mates.

Ducks and geese flying in formation also do so to save group energy and provide safety. Military aircraft on a tactical mission fly in a formation for mutual support, mission integrity, better navigation, and penetrating bad weather. These are also keys to classroom and organizational success.

It is difficult to get a man to understand something when his salary depends on him not understanding it.

- Upton Sinclair

In the Workplace and in Life, you get the behavior that you reward.

- Dad

You'll get better cooperation and results if you are sincerely interested in people's families and interests, not simply in how they do their job.

- Coach John Wooden

No matter how much time you've wasted in the past, you still have an entire today.

- Denis Waitley

To increase your effectiveness constantly ask yourself, "Am I being Productive or am I being Busy?"

- Dad

Many persons invest heavily of their time and money in trainings and materials to gain knowledge only to have the "learning" gather dust on the shelves of "inactivity". To Know is to Do.

- Dad

3 A's?

Attend the Crucial Few and Ignore the Trivial Many.

- Dad

Choose actions appropriately.
In flood-prone areas replace chickens with ducks.

- Dad

If you are building a house and the nail breaks, do you stop building, or do you change the nail?

- Rwandan Proverb

Something not working does not mean something is not going to work.

- Stephen Pierce

Every Job is an Opportunity and a Challenge. Make it "So" and it will be "So".

- Dad

If you are selling eggs, don't piss-off your chickens.

- Anonymous

Be watchful of creating felonies out of matters not worth a summons.

- Dan Barry

3 A's?

Give me six hours to chop down a tree and I will spend the first four sharpening the axe.

- Abraham Lincoln

You must have long-range goals to keep you from short-range failures.

- Charles C. Noble

Communication is the Response you get.

- Marshall Thurber

Problems are not stop signs, they are guidelines.

- Robert Schuller

Always watch your "six". (180 degrees behind you)

- Pilot's Law

3 A's?

Razor Burn

I was a college freshman sitting in a barber's chair with an unsightly and irritating case of facial razor burn. The barber asked, "Why do you shave so close?" I replied, "I want a very smooth face."

The wise barber counseled, "Don't you realize that no matter how closely you shave today, tomorrow you are going to have to do it again?"

That day was my last case of razor burn. The larger lesson was not wasted either. The greatest lesson arrived when I contemplated the corollary of his advice, "What are some issues that need to be <u>done</u> well because you may not return to them timely, or ever?"

I made a listing:
- First meetings
- Table manners
- Term papers / Exams
- Timely Thank You's
- Timely sincere acknowledgements
- Personally important race

Since then I have added to my list:

- Monthly reports
- Public statements especially issued during times of crisis
- Press interviews
- Crisis decisions
- Leadership meetings
- Any decision affecting the well-being of another
- Farewells
- Termination interviews

What would you add?

Many from my list are related to engagement with others. This is a useful alert. Being alert is to be conscious, present, and attentive while engaging with others are key skills of effective Responsible Leadership.

Most time is wasted, not in hours, but in minutes. A bucket with a small hole in the bottom gets just as empty as a bucket that is deliberately kicked over.

- Paul J. Meyer

Minutes are worth more than money, spend them wisely.

- Thomas P. Murphy

Must maintain and sustain to remain.

- Dad

Never settle for the cards you are dealt – but while you are working to earn new ones, learn to play the ones you have.

- Dad

4 P's necessary for Success:

Prayer
Productivity
Perseverance
Patience

There's a myth that time is money. In fact, time is more precious than money. It's a nonrenewable resource. Once you've spent it, and if you've spent it badly, it's gone forever.

- Neil Fiore

3 A's?

The Treasure Cave Theory of Leadership

In the mid-80's, I was a contractor to the US government in the former Panama Canal Zone. I had hundreds of local employees. Among them were half-dozen Embera Choco Indian tribesmen who hailed from the foreboding Darien jungle. The Darien, connecting Panama and Columbia, was virtually impenetrable and was the only stretch of land between the northern tip of Alaska and the southern tip of Chile where the Inter-American Highway was not connected.

The father of these 'Indios' was a Choco Cacique (Chief) and also a Brujo (Witch-Doctor) of their village. The Chief visited me on several occasions bringing stories of gold and ancient Spanish treasures that he had discovered near his very small jungle village. The Cacique told me of finding a secret cave within which he uncovered a large wooden door. Behind the door he found a six-foot long alligator statue made of gold and many Spanish Conquistador helmets. Remember in the 1500's, the Spanish Conquistadors, which plundered Inca gold and treasures from Peru, traversed the land bridge of Panama exiting on the Caribbean coast to board their ships for return voyages to Spain.

My interest and thoughts of adventure and riches spiked.

The Cacique said that he would guide me to his cave and share his findings. He asked me to bring provisions to his village of 40 people; shotgun and .22 shells, matches, rice, beans, coffee, beer, cigarettes—and bolts of red *tela* (cloth).

The Cacique cautioned that the area surrounding the cave was patrolled by dangerous 'devil dogs'. The *tela* would be used to safely cordon off the cave, as the devil dogs feared the bright red cloth.

Within two weeks I had convinced several equally excited friends to join me in this treasure reclaiming expedition.

At 05:00 on a Saturday morning we left Panama City with a convoy of two of my large flatbed trucks and two 4-wheel drive vehicles. The journey to the end of the paved road to the beginning of the Darien was to take only three hours.

Not so! Mechanical failures and multiple tire blowouts delayed our arrival to 18:00. Near the equator, in the jungle, at 6:00 PM darkness is 'at hand'.

The planned Choco bearers who were to help carry all the provisions and gear to the village had long ago decided that we were 'No-Shows' and had left for their village. This meant that the five Gringos, my friends, and me had to carry all the gear.

The Darien jungle is not a welcoming place for the inexperienced trekker.

At night it is a black scary a place.

Barely able to see three feet in front, each burdened with more than 50 lbs. of gear, my team stumbled blindly through the jungle while we fearfully followed the sole Choco guide for over three hours – that felt more like three days. If there was a path we couldn't see it. An unspoken rule was not to mention the deadly snakes, crocs, or wild boar that lived in the jungle

3 A's?

Finally we broke out of the jungle onto a riverbank. Three 20-foot cayucos (dug-out canoes) were waiting for us. Loading and boarding the narrow cayucos required balance and caution. Each dugout was piloted by an Choco whose only propulsion was a long pole. My team and I did not want to know what kind of river-life threatened us from below.

Two hours later, exhausted, we disembarked on a small beach at the entrance to the Cacique's village. Dragging all the gear up the slope to the village our only aim was to collapse in whatever fashion of beds were available.

Not to be! The Cacique and a few elders had prepared a welcoming ceremony. Due to the very late time he immediately began. My team and I sat on the floor of the Cacique's raised hut while he began chanting to honor us and bless the expedition. The chanting, accompanied by the elders' drumming, lasted two hours – it felt like two days!

My attempt to meditate to the chanting was really more dozing, on and off. Each dozing would lead to full-colored fanciful dreams.

After less than four hours of restless sleep rude roosters brazenly crowed a wake-up call, "No choice. Get-up!" Still exhausted we surveyed our surroundings in the daylight. The village consisted of a dozen thatched-roofed, open-sided huts built on stilts. The huts were raised about 10 feet in the air to provide safety from roaming predators and floods.

After a simple breakfast of fertilized eggs and yucca, aided by some gear-carrying villagers, including bare-breasted teenage girls, we formed single-file and set off hiking through the jungle.

Our hike, steamy hot in daylight, was punctuated with annoying attacks of all sorts of flying insects, leeches, and other creepy crawlers. After 1-1/2 hours we arrived at a small clearing in the center of which was a 10 feet deep pit about 20 feet around. The Cacique pointed to a small opening on the other side of the pit and exclaimed, "Aqui estamos!" – "We are here!", or something like that in his native language signaling that this was the site of the treasure cave.

My friends and I jumped in the pit and peered into the opening. With our flashlights we could see that the three-foot wide and tall entrance opened into a cavern with a five-foot ceiling and an indeterminable depth. Our lights also revealed that the cave ceiling was crowded with thousands of hanging bats – the floor with inches of bat droppings. The ammonia smell was nearly over-powering.

The Cacique handed us shovels and invited us to enter the cave. Some of my team members balked. No braver than the rest but compelled as the expedition financier and organizer I crawled, shovel in hand, through the entrance. A son of the Chief accompanied me and told me to start digging on the far earthen cave wall. So I did. The bats didn't like my presence any more than I did theirs and they made it known by swooping and darting down at me. As the cave ceiling was only five feet high I had to dig while crouching on my knees trying not to touch or be touched by the bats.

Every 30 minute or so I would exit the cave for a rest and invite others to share in the digging. No takers...

After many hours of digging, finding only more dirt I exited the cave and asked the Cacique where the large wooden door was. In his language he made a lengthy reply gesturing wildly. I patiently waited for the fractured translation from Choco to Spanish to English.

Poof! That's how epiphanies happen! Mine was when I finally understood that the large wooden door, the golden alligator, and the Conquistador helmets were all seen by the Cacique/Brujo in a 'Vision'!
I am certain that the untold part of his vision included rifle shells, rice, beans, coffee, beer, cigarettes – and tela!

What is the lesson here?

An effective leader always works to understand the needs and wants of people feeding him information – knowing this will affect the 'What, Where, Why, and How' of the info provided and that the intentions and goals may not be in mutual alignment. Effective leaders do not let their personal exuberance cloud their judgment when developing or executing plans.

I would tell this long story to my managers and supervisors mentoring them to exercise diligence in assessing the needs, wants, and motivations of our suppliers and even our clients – working for alignment before finalizing or implementing deliverables.

What possible activities in your personal or professional life might be succumbing to not practicing the lessons of The Treasure Cave Theory of Leadership?

Name three. What reassessed actions are you going to take?

Never waste an experience of extreme stress, ego-wrenching embarrassment, or personal injury without learning from it.

- Dad

Leadership responsibility is to "Walk the Talk" – not play "Stumble the Mumble".

- Anonymous

Think fast. Talk slow.

- Anonymous

The inevitable end of multiple chiefs is that they fade and disappear for lack of unity.

- Napolean Bonaparte

If you can't measure it you don't understand it.

- Arthur Jones

Lighthouse Theory of Leadership

(The names and places have been changed to protect the guilty.)

Perched on the high observation deck of a lighthouse, bathed by cooling trade winds, I looked out from the mountaintop of this small,-undeveloped Caribbean island toward the mainland. This was one of my favorite places on earth. To the north and east were thousands of miles of the Atlantic. To the south and west, I viewed the mountains and jungle of this beautiful Central American country.

The spectacular vista and experience was enhanced by the journey to arrive atop this lighthouse. I had to travel for many hours to reach the mainland coast. The last hour required a four-wheel drive vehicle to navigate the pitted and neglected unpaved roads. At the coast, I would transfer all my gear to a cayuco, a dugout canoe, for a 40-minute voyage to the island. The cayuco was beached in the shallows 50 meters from dry land. I would again gather all my gear and wade through the knee-deep water to the shore.

As there were no vehicles on the island, getting to the isolated and unattended lighthouse required more than an hour's hike along the shore, through a small village, along a narrow path through the hot dense jungle, while continually climbing to reach the mountain peak on which the lighthouse was located. Hot, sweaty, and tired, I was rewarded with refreshing breezes when breaking-out of the jungle and into the clearing surrounding the lighthouse. This relief was temporary as, packing all gear and supplies (leaving them would result in them being carried off or pilfered by the lurking monkeys or wild boars) I would climb the 132 steps up the circular staircase inside the hot, humid, and dark tower of the Lighthouse. The stairs finally emptied into the round, window-filled room housing the large powerful light mechanism. This light would project its beams nightly warning sailors of the dangerous rocks, corals, and shallows surrounding the island.

My ideal spot, after traversing the ruts, waves, jungle, and mountain climb, was a perch on the outside deck encircling the light-room. For me, the splendid view and breeze was worth the journey. In truth, the journey greatly enhanced the experience.

Not so for the lighthouse workers. They too had to make the same arduous journey, carrying large buckets of paint, cleaning, and maintenance gear by hand. All these had to be schlepped, through the jungle, up the hills, and finally up the narrow challenging lighthouse staircase. Their job was to clean and paint the inside of the light room and maintain the light mechanism to ward off the corrosive effects of the salty sea-air. Most of the time, the job was given to a lone unsupervised worker.

In the 10+ years that I would visit the Lighthouse, I noticed increasingly shabby maintenance—the windows became spackled with drips of paint from careless painters addressing the metal window frames. An ever-thickening film of grime and paint began to overtake clear viewing through the windows. Although I noticed with some concern for this negligence, my primary focus was always to go outside to sit on the deck and refresh my body and spirit.

On one of my last trips to 'my' lighthouse, I was met by some local islanders who told me a story about a boat which had recently crashed on some nearby rocks, seriously injuring a number of the sailors. In researching the incident, I found that the primary cause of the crash was believed to be that the lighthouse beam was dimmed and refracted due to the dirty, paint-film covered windows and so did not properly illuminate the dangerous area.

What's the Leadership moral of the story?

"A 'watched pot' won't boil over. - A responsible effective leader can delegate the work – but he cannot delegate the oversight."

In my many leadership roles while serving in developing countries where I was not conversant in the local language, I would coach and mentor my subordinates with stories embedded with management and leadership principles. The Lighthouse Theory of Leadership was always one that was effective in bringing home the requirement for active oversight and supervision, to promote correct task accomplishment and to prevent any potential undesirable consequences, especially for unpleasant tasks.

What responsibilities or assignments do you have where the LTL applies?

What gets measured gets managed.

- Peter Drucker

Not everything that can be counted counts, and not everything that counts can be counted.

- Albert Einstein

Don't judge each day by the harvest you reap, but by the seeds you plant.

- Robert Louis Stevenson

One of the great mistakes is to judge policies and programs by their intentions rather than their results.

- Milton Friedman

Every person who gets rich by competition knocks down the ladder by which he rises, and keeps others down, but every person who gets rich by creation opens a way for the others to follow and inspires them to do so.

- Wallace D. Wattles

There is a big difference between what you have a right to do and what is right to do.

- Dad

People who buy a ¼ drill bit don't necessarily want a drill bit – they want a ¼ hole. Always look to learn what is really wanted and needed and work to give it.

- Dad

The B-52 Theory of Leadership

The Boeing B-52 Stratofortress, affectionately nicknamed the BUFF (Big Ugly Flying F**ker) by pilots, entered the USAF inventory during the early period of the 'Cold War' with the former Soviet Union. The B-52, a significant deterrent element of the US 'Cold War' strategy, was designed as a high-altitude strategic bombing platform for delivering nuclear weapons. In my early active air Force service in the Strategic Air Command (SAC) I was a 'right-seater' in the BUFF.

The eight-engine BUFF, with a wingspan of 190 feet and a gross weight of 450,000 lbs., was designed to fly into a target area at an altitude in excess of 40,000 feet. Aircraft detection radars in the 50's were 'line-of-sight' and had limited ranges. These were deemed incapable of timely detecting a high-speed intruding aircraft at 40,000 feet.

However technology intervened. In mid-1960, former USAF Captain Gary Powers, while piloting a USAF/CIA U-2 reconnaissance jet aircraft, at an altitude of 80,000 feet, was shot down by a Soviet missile.

The message was clear. The strategy for the BUFF to perform its mission at 40,000' was now obsolete given the greatly improved Soviet radar technology.

The problem became, "How do you make a multi-million dollar aircraft, designed for a specific mission, a pillar of US deterrence, to be still effective with a now ineffective delivery strategy? You can't redesign the aircraft. What's left? The 'strategy'.

SAC leadership decided to severely change the strategy of flying as high as possible to fly as low and fast as possible when penetrating hostile territory. The new strategy required the BUFF to fly at Mach .86 at 250 feet AGL (Above Ground Level). Remember the Buff's wingspan was 190 feet! Hugging the ground lower than most hills and some buildings enabled the BUFF to avoid early detection – and for the pilots and crew made for some exciting flying!

What's the Leadership lesson here?

> *Plan well. Follow your strategy. When events make it clear that the strategy is ineffective - change immediately. Resources of hardware and personnel are usually not timely changeable. Their use might be. Adapt, Redeploy, Proceed.*

Effective Leadership constantly reviews events and conditions – continually adapting their resources and use.

3 A's?

Where might you be stuck by applying ineffective strategies to accomplish your goals?

List three areas that are currently not working for you and as Henry Ford said, "Don't find fault. Find a solution."

No problem can be solved from the same level of consciousness that created it.

- Albert Einstein

To retain your "self-respect" it is better to displease some people by doing what you know is right than to temporarily please them by doing what you know is wrong.

- William J. Boetcker

7 Habits of Highly Effective People

Habit 1: Be Proactive
Habit 2: Begin with the End in Mind
Habit 3: Put First Things First
Habit 4: Think Win/Win
Habit 5: Seek First to Understand, Then to Be Understood
Habit 6: Synergize
Habit 7: Sharpen the Saw

- Stephen Covey

Conduct is what we do; character is what we are. Character is the root of the tree; conduct is the fruit it bears.

- E. M. Bounds

To know how to do something is skill.
To know why to do something is wisdom.
To know when to do something is judgment.
To know to strive to do your best is dedication.
To do it for the benefit of others is compassion.
To get the job done is achievement.
To do this quietly is humility.

To get others to do all of these things willingly is leadership.

- Anonymous

Ability can take you to the top, but it takes character to keep you there.

- Zig Ziglar

A single stroke of an ax will not fell a tree – but many will.

- Spanish Proverb

Inspiring leadership often requires being tough – not willing to compromise with mediocrity.

- Walter Isaacson

Management is efficiency in climbing the ladder of success; leadership is determining whether the ladder is leaning against the right wall.

-Stephen Covey

3 A's?

Example is not the main thing in influencing others. It is the only thing.

- Albert Schweitzer

The mediocre teacher (leader) tells.
The good teacher (leader) explains.
The superior teacher (leader) demonstrates.
The great teacher (leader) inspires.

- William Arthur Ward
* (parenthesis – mine)

Great leaders are like baseball umpires; they go practically unnoticed when doing their job right.

- Byrd Baggett

OODA Loop

- Observe

- Orient

- Decide

- Act

US Air Force Management template

OODA Loop is a concept originally applied to the combat operations process, often at the strategic level in military operations. It is now also often applied to understand commercial operations and learning processes.

The concept was developed by military strategist and USAF Colonel John Boyd.

Notes
Record some of your own insights and decisions here

Set your sights high, the higher the better.
Expect the most wonderful things to happen,
not in the future but right now.
Realize that nothing is too good.
Allow absolutely nothing to hamper you
or hold you up in any way.

- Eileen Caddy

I am thankful to all those who said NO to me.
It's because of them I did it myself.

- Albert Einstein

Chapter XII

SUCCESS
(Mission Accomplished)

Be all that you can be.

                                        - US Army

Do all that you can do.

                                - Anonymous

Although thoughtful planning precedes success, planning that supplants doing locks in inertia. Hoping is not a strategy. Waiting for just the right time is like eagerly waiting for the delivery man and then refusing to answer the door when he comes.

Remember, changing your thinking is only the first step in changing your life. Life changes only occur when we change our doing.

How you define success has a large impact on your motivation. For me, success has never been just a private victory. Success always required lifting up the aspirations, achievements, and well-being of others also. How would it feel being the richest most accomplished person standing alone on the moon?

Engineering for the greater well-being of others is the surest way to leverage for your own success.

Also as an additional endorsement of the wisdom of *Small Bites*, Oriental philosopher, Hang Sen, said,

> *Man who listens to wisdom of many masters takes shortcut to success.*

Mission Accomplished

To be successful you need to "kick butt, take names, create change" – passiveness is not a virtue. Change requires courageously challenging the status quo.

- Dad

Magic ingredients of Achievement
- Inspiration
- Dedication
- Perspiration

- Dad

Achievement Test: Outcomes are more important than Intentions. Does a given plan or action arouse energy, foster skills, spur social mobility, connectivity, and support, help you to favorably transform your life and others around you?

- Dad

Take action to ensure that Not Now's do not become Never Will's.
- Dad

If one advances confidently in the direction of his dreams, and endeavors to have the life that he has imagined, he will meet with a success unexpected in common hours.

- Henry David Thoreau

3 A's?

A professional is one who can do his best work when he doesn't feel like it.

- Alfred Alistair Cooke

Winners never quit and quitters never win.

- Vince Lombardi

Greatness is not found in possessions, power, position, or prestige.
It is discovered in goodness, humility, service, and character.

- William Arthur Ward

I firmly believe that any man's finest hour, the greatest fulfillment of all that he holds dear, is the moment when he has worked his heart out in a good cause and lies exhausted on the field of battle-victorious.

- Vince Lombardi

The process of "Triumphing over Tragedy" is its own reward.

- Anonymous

What you do today can improve all your tomorrows.

- Ralph Marston

When you quit striving to get better – you don't.

- Dad

On road to success – your mission is to keep going.

- Anonymous

He who is not courageous enough to take risks will accomplish nothing in life.

- Muhammad Ali

Big shots are only little shots who keep shooting.

- Christopher D. Morley

The future belongs to those who believe in the beauty of their dream.

- Eleanor Roosevelt

Dream Big Dreams – and remember "Pursuit" is the Key to Happiness.

- Dad

The difference between a successful person and others is not a lack of strength, not a lack of knowledge, but rather in a lack of will.

- Vince Lombardi

It's good to take on "God-sized" tasks, so when we achieve it we know who deserves the credit.

- Jonathan Reckford

3 A's?

Only passions, great passions, can elevate the soul to great things.
- Dennis Diderot

Find great joy and satisfaction in life when doing what people say you cannot do.
- Dad

Work to earn what you pray for.
- Anonymous

Happiness, health, and prosperity do not occur by accident.
- Brian Tracy

You can have anything you want if you help enough people get what they want.
- Dad

All riches have their origin in mind. Wealth is in ideas - not money.
- Robert Collier

Success is not an accident. Be prepared to make continual course corrections.
- Dad

If you have the courage to begin, you have the courage to succeed.

- David Viscott

On Success: You must be interested in finding the best way, not in having your own way.

- Coach John Wooden

If you want to succeed you should strike out on new paths, rather than travel the worn paths of accepted success.

- John D. Rockefeller

Success is neither magical nor mysterious. Success is the natural consequence of consistently applying basic fundamentals.

- Jim Rohn

Success in any endeavor does not happen by accident. Rather, it's the result of deliberate decisions, conscious effort, and immense persistence... all directed at specific goals.

- Gary Ryan Blair

Success is nothing more than a few simple disciplines, practiced every day; while failure is simply a few errors in judgment, repeated every day. It is the accumulative weight of our disciplines and our judgments that leads us to either.

- Jim Rohn

If you want to achieve "peak" performance you can't "try" when you compete. You need to let it happen – chuck it out there.

- Terry Bradshaw

One person with a commitment is worth a hundred who only have an interest.

- Mary Crowley

There is only one way to succeed in anything, and that is to give everything. I do and I demand that my players do.

- Vince Lombardi

Most beginnings are small, and appear trivial and insignificant, but in reality they are the most important things in life.

- James Allen

Best Defense is a good Offense,

- Anonymous

Limitations live only in our minds. But if we use our imaginations, our possibilities become limitless.

- Jamie Paolinetti

If it's your job to eat a frog, it's best to do it first thing in the morning. And If it's your job to eat two frogs, it's best to eat the biggest one first.

- Mark Twain

3 A's?

A winner is someone who recognizes his God-given talents, works his tail off to develop them into skills, and uses these skills to accomplish his goals.

- Larry Bird

A successful person is one who can lay a firm foundation with the bricks that others throw at him or her.

- David Brinkley

If you spend five minutes complaining, you have just wasted five minutes. If you continue complaining, it won't be long before they haul you out to a financial desert and there let you choke on the dust of your own regret.

- Jim Rohn

The secret of success is you have to separate your excuses from your goals.

- Sean Stephenson

Life is what we make it. Always has been, always will be.

- Grandma Moses

Hard work spotlights the character of people: some turn up their sleeves, some turn up their noses, and some don't turn up at all.

- Sam Ewing

3 A's?

What you get by achieving your goals is not as important as what you become by achieving your goals.

- Henry David Thoreau

You cannot prove that you cannot create the business (life) of your dreams – you can only prove that you haven't done it yet.

- Stephen Pierce
* (parenthesis insert is mine)

To achieve great things, two things are needed; a plan, and not quite enough time.

- Leonard Bernstein

Strive not to be a success, but rather to be of value.

- Albert Einstein

It is better to travel well than to arrive.

- Gautama Buddha

The journey is the reward.

- Steve Jobs

If you have integrity, nothing else matters. If you don't have integrity, nothing else matters.

- Alan Simpson

Success is failure turned inside out -
The silver tint of the clouds of doubt,
And you never can tell how close you are -
It may be near when it seems afar;
So stick to the fight when you're hardest hit -
It's when things seem worst that you mustn't quit.

- Anonymous

Life is a Garden. Dig it!

- from the film Joe Dirt

Before you speak, listen.
Before you write, think.
Before you spend, earn.
Before you invest, investigate.
Before you criticize, wait.
Before you pray, forgive.
Before you quit, try.
Before you retire, save.
Before you die, give.

- William Arthur Ward

3 A's?

Beyond the Winning

Beyond the Winning and the Goal,
Beyond the Glory and the Fame,
I feel a Flame within my Soul
Born by the Spirit of the Game.

And where the Barriers wait
As raised by the Opposing gods,
I find a Thrill in bucking Fate
And riding down the endless Odds.

Where others wither in the Fire
Or fall behind with some raw mishap,
Where others lag behind and tire
And break beneath the Handicap

I find a new and deeper Thrill
To take Me into the uphill Spin
For the Test is greater still
And Something that I revel in!

- Grantland Rice

3 A's?

Notes
Record some of your own insights and decisions here

The key is to keep company only with people who uplift you,
whose presence calls forth your best.

- Epictetus

Chapter XIII

FAMILY & FRIENDS
(Air Crew)

The quality of your life is in direct proportion to the quality of your relationships.

- Anthony Robbins

If you associate with turkeys you will never fly with eagles.

- Brian Tracy

One of my mentors has continually reinforced the principle that it doesn't matter where you go in life, what you do...it's who you have beside you. Most times we don't choose our family, yet these persons, who care most for us, usually provide the experiential laboratory for what works and what doesn't in human relationships. Nurturing and supporting these relationships are key components to our sense of responsibility and service.

We do have choice in choosing our friends. Making good choices is one of the most important things we can do. The choices we make and how we cultivate and care for these relationships largely determine the success and joy that we experience.

As stated previously, "If you always live with those that are lame, you yourself will learn to limp." Conversely if you surround yourself with persons of integrity, industry, and compassion you will most likely become an active member of a powerful and successful group.

Operating Philosophy

My operating philosophy is to practice "Clear-eyed Optimism". I believe that most people are good. I believe that the overall impact of this philosophy promotes greater opportunities for joy and perceived Universal support.

The few times when I lapsed into an unenlightened and shallow version of this belief, I allowed a person to undermine my success and cause me grief. The grief would likely have been greatly mitigated had I illuminated the relationship by closer observation of the other's needs and more clearly sussed out their intentions.

The French scientist and philosopher, Blaise Pascal, cautions,

The heart has its reasons which reason knows not of.

My experience has taught me that everyone primarily sees facts from their own perceived best interest, often narrowly defined. This is not to suggest that being a cynic is preferable, but that "clear-seeing", allowing that everyone does not share the full "do unto others" operating philosophy, requires my full attention. I must be alert not to confuse personality and charisma with enlightened mutual or public interest. The caution, "Don't do business with strangers" applies to all of our relationships, even relatives.

While a full vetting of a stranger's intentions is usually not possible, I've found that an optimistic "eyes-wide-open" approach is most revealing. Detecting attempts at duplicity or manipulation is easier when I have invited a person into relationship. A "clear-eyed" relationship, whether with stranger, friend, or family, always starts and ends with effective communication.

Have you ever encountered a person who is so wrapped up in their own thoughts and interests that they allow no time for yours?

Sometime ago I met a person who was quite accomplished, and very full of themselves. He went on and on describing in detail his thoughts and feelings, not stopping to consider mine. When he finally did, his questions took the form of, "Enough about me. Tell me about you. What do you think about me?"

What would your experience in this communication cycle be? Aren't they still a stranger with unvetted intentions if there is no two-way dialogue? How eager are you to continue the one-way conversation? How eager are you to enter into a business or other relationship?

Stephen Covey's Habit # 5, his principle for empathetic communication from his wonderful book The 7 habits of Highly Effective People, is, Seek First to Understand, Then to be Understood. Simply: don't prescribe without diagnosis. Covey further counsels, Unless you're influenced by my uniqueness, I am not going to be influenced by your advice.

My personal formula for Effective Communication and Relationships is:
A R A C
- A = Acknowledgement
- R = Respect
- A = Appreciation
- C = Consideration

- Always start with properly Acknowledging a person's presence. This immediately opens the door for exchange.
- The default position of a new relationship is Respect. Although trust must be earned, initial respect should be granted.
- Genuine Appreciation for another's presence and gifts, real and potential, is a blessing to the receiver, and the giver.
- Consideration is an external expression of A, R, A. It can be a physical exchange, an appropriate courtesy, a timely follow-up, being a thoughtful listener, or as an earnest deliberator.

My formula is practiced with attempt to first focus on the other's perspective, but with "eyes-wide-open". My goal is to establish a mutually beneficial relationship based on mutual respect and appreciation. This must become innate for effective Responsible Leadership.

Try this formula first with your family. They may not be the easiest communication partners, but the rewards are the greatest.

Air Crew

In everyone's life, at some time, our inner fire goes out. It is then burst into flame by an encounter with another human being. We should all be thankful for those people who rekindle the inner spirit.

- Albert Schweitzer

Giving acknowledgment and service to family and others reinforces your connection with the Divine.

- Dad

Friendship makes prosperity more shinning and lessens adversity by dividing and sharing it.

- Cicero

To the Soul there is hardly anything more healing than "friendship".

- Thomas Moore

With children, we have the opportunity to cultivate patience and humor, deepen the intelligence of the heart, learn to find hidden riches in ordinary life, and unexpected happiness.

- Piero Ferrucci

The most called-upon prerequisite of a friend is an accessible ear.

- Maya Angelou

Children pay little attention to their parents' teachings, but reproduce their characters faithfully.

- Mason Cooley

Grief can take care of itself, but to get the full value of a joy, you must have somebody to divide it with.

- Mark Twain

Be careful the environment you choose for it will shape you; be careful the friends you choose for you will become like them.

- W. Clement Stone

The key is to keep company only with people who uplift you, whose presence calls forth your best.

- Epictetus

While the roots of happiness from individual success may be shallow, the bonds from loving, mutually supportive relationships are transforming.

- Dad

The quality of your life is in direct proportion to the quality of your relationships.

- Anthony Robbins

Friendship... is not something you learn in school. But if you haven't learned the meaning of friendship, you really haven't learned anything.

- Muhammad Ali

When we dream alone it is only a dream. When we dream with others, it is the beginning of reality.

- Dom Helder Camara

The slave has but one master - the ambitious man has many as can help in making his fortune.

- Jean de La Bruyere

Notes
Record some of your own insights and decisions here

©Silverander, EthnoGraphic

We make a living by what we get,
but we make a life by what we give.

- Norman MacEwan

Chapter XIV

SERVICE
(Crew Care)

No one can create joy, peace of mind, or fulfillment for us. Our first job is to create the conditions that allow them to occur. After safety and security these conditions must include a positive sense of personal gratitude and growth, family and social contributions, and others' appreciation. For me, these *Small Bites*, as action steps, have contributed to the creation of these conditions.

When you are a wise and responsible person you don't just choose those things that feel good or that you want to do. You choose those that have an impact on your greater well-being and that of your family and community.

True Joy

There is one True Joy in life; that is, being used for a Purpose recognized by Yourself as a worthy one.

Being a Force of Nature, not just a feverish selfish little clod of ailments and grievances complaining that the World does not devote itself to you – to making you happy.

I am of the opinion that my Life belongs to the Whole Community – and it is my Privilege – My Privilege to do for it whatever I can. For the harder I work the more I live.

I want to be thoroughly used up when I die. Life is no brief candle to me. It is like a Brilliant Torch that I have a hold of for the moment and I will make it burn ever more brightly as I pass it on to future generations.

- George Bernard Shaw

Crew Care

You are not here merely to make a living. You are here in order to enable the world to live more amply, with greater vision, with a finer spirit of hope and achievement. You are here to enrich the world, and you impoverish yourself if you forget the errand.
- Woodrow Wilson

It has been said, The second half of your life ought to be for significance. What if you lived the first half of your life making significant contributions to your family and community?
- Dad

There are two ways of spreading light: to be the candle or the mirror that reflects it.
- Edith Wharton

Never hesitate to put out your hand; never hesitate to accept the outstretched hand of another.
- Pope John Paul XXIII

Giving connects two people, the giver and the receiver, and this connection gives birth to a new sense of belonging.
- Deepak Chopra

To get joy, we must give it, and to keep joy, we must scatter it.
- John Templeton

3 A's?

When we feel love and kindness toward others, it not only makes others feel loved and cared for, but it helps us also to develop inner happiness and peace.

- His Holiness, the Dalai Lama

Love and kindness are never wasted. They always make a difference. They bless the one who receives them, and they bless you, the giver.

- Barbara De Angelis

Sometimes when you sacrifice something precious, you're not really losing it. You're just passing it on to someone else.

- Mitch Albom

As "God" is "Life Force", the Creator, Organizer, Sustainer of everything, then loving God and seeing God in all Others requires attitudes and actions that support Life.

- Dad

Only those who have learned the power of sincere and selfless contribution experience life's deepest joy: true fulfillment.

- Anthony Robbins

The Bridge Builder

An old man, going a lone highway,
Came, at the evening, cold and gray,
To a chasm, vast, and deep, and wide,
Through which was flowing a swollen tide.

The old man crossed in the twilight dim;
The swollen stream had no fear for him;
But he turned, when safe on the other side,
And built a bridge to span the tide.

"Old man," said a fellow pilgrim, near,
"You are wasting strength with building here;
Your journey will end with the ending day;
You never again will pass this way;
You've crossed the chasm, deep and wide-
Why build you this bridge at the evening tide?"

The Builder lifted his old gray head:
"Good friend, in the path I have come," he said,
"There followeth after me today,
A youth, whose feet must pass this way.
This chasm, that has been naught to me,
To that fair-haired youth may a pitfall be.
He, too, may cross in the twilight dim;
Good friend, I am building this bridge for him."

- Will Allen Dromgoole

3 A's?

One Stroke at a Time

Floating lazily on my back in the Aegean Sea, I was drifting in and out of a pre-planned reverie. Three weeks earlier my son, Gary, had been born. He was healthy and beautiful.

The many weeks before had been less so. The doctors had advised that the baby was in a breech position and a cesarean delivery was recommended and scheduled.

On week before the scheduled surgery, Gary had flipped inside and a normal birth was now possible. With labor pains commencing, my wife, Marlena, was taken to the hospital. While monitoring Marlena's labor, it became evident that the baby was under stress as his heart rate had become irregular. The doctor, fearing that the umbilical cord had become wrapped around Gary's neck, decided to perform an immediate cesarean. The doctor's assessment and decision were correct - indeed the cord had wrapped dangerously around Gary's neck.

In addition to the normal stresses preceding the birth of a child my work and travel schedule had also sponsored mounting stresses. With Gary and Marlena healthy and safe, three weeks later I headed to the island of Phuket for a three-day respite.

Back to the Aegean: My floating reverie collapsed quickly when I opened my eyes to discover that a rip-tide had swept me hundreds of yard from shore. Never a strong swimmer, I attempted to swallow my panic and swim toward land. Not to be!

3 A's?

The more I thrashed, the farther I was carried out to sea. I could barely spot a few people on the beach. My yells for help were unnoticed and unattended. Panic began to take control.

My total thoughts were about my new son and how thoughtless and careless I had been to deprive him of my fathering, and me of his loving companionship. From a deep recess a memory emerged.

I recalled reading that you cannot 'swim against the tide'. To overcome the pull of the tide required swimming at an angle with it, hoping to swim out of its grip.

My thoughts exploded in expletives, "Damn! If this life experience is going to end here it is going to watch me swimming—and swimming!" Silently, but vehemently, I shouted down my panic and replaced it with the resolve that my life and Gary's, and all my loved ones, were worth 'one more stroke'! My physical and mental strength became irrelevant, as did Time. My total focus was 'one more stroke'! No enlightenment or 'open heavens' embraced me. I swam and I swam, and I swam—'one stroke at a time'.

A million years later I sensed that the current no longer commanded me. I turned toward shore, now a couple of miles distant, and continued one stroke at a time.

Stroke by stroke I inched closer to shore. I swam, promising to re-unite with my loved ones. The water warmed as it shallowed. Trembling, I

3 A's?

finally stood, staggered to the beach, seeing children and parents frolicking, totally oblivious of my survival ordeal.

As I collapsed on the bed of the rented island cottage, several thoughts flooded my mind:

1. Sometimes we seem to be truly alone.
2. Yet, we have inner strengths unbeknown to us.
3. The power of Love is a doorway.
4. As I create my life, great opportunities and contributions are possible when I willfully demand access to these strengths.
5. Summoned strength may not rush forth. It may only appear when you are decisively acting 'one stroke at a time'.
6. My life experience is blessed, it is my challenge to share my strengths for the benefit of others.

This story could have been positioned in my chapters on Adversity, Courage, Success, or even Responsibility. I chose Service because the lesson for me is, "I am strengthened when working for the benefit of my loved ones and others.

Although not always living-up to my own expectations, my life mantra continues to be, "Serving self is in serving others – one stroke at a time."

"The service we render to others is really the rent we pay for our room on this earth. It is obvious that man is himself a traveler; that the purpose of this world is not 'to have and to hold' but 'to give and serve.' There can be no other meaning."
- Sir Wilfred Grenfell

There are those who give with joy, and that joy is their reward.
- Kahlil Gibran

We make a living by what we get, but we make a life by what we give.
- Norman MacEwan

It's not what you gather, but what you scatter that tells what kind of life you have lived!!
- Anonymous

The best way to cheer yourself up is to try to cheer somebody else up.
- Mark Twain

We get what we Give – and Giving is the best part of Getting.
- Anonymous

Let us not be weary in doing good; for at the proper time we will reap a harvest if we do not give up. Therefore, as we have the op-portunity, let us do good to all people.
- Galatians 6: 9-10

Man becomes great exactly in the degree in which he works for the welfare of his fellow-men.
- Mohandas Gandhi

3 A's?

The charity that is a trifle to us can be precious to others.

- Homer

Kindness is the language which the deaf can hear and the blind can see.

- Mark Twain

Wise sayings often fall on barren ground, but a kind word is never thrown away.

- Arthur Helps

In this life we cannot always do great things. We can only do small things with great love.

- Mother Teresa

If you can't do it all – do what you can.

- www.foundationforabetterlife.com

Whoever renders service to many puts himself in line for greatness - great wealth, great return, great satisfaction, great reputation and great joy.

- Jim Rohn

You can't help someone get up a hill without getting closer to the top yourself.

- H. Norman Schwarzkopf

Look for opportunities this year to make a significant long-term, positive impact on the lives of others. The best way to feel good is to be good.

- Michael Josephson

There is a wonderful mythical law of nature that the three things we crave most in life—Happiness, Freedom, and Peace of Mind -- are always attained by giving them to someone else.

- Peyton Conway

Do all the good you can. By all the means you can. In all the places you can. At all times you can. As long as ever you can.

- John Wesley

If you want happiness for an hour - take a nap.
If you want happiness for a day - go fishing.
If you want happiness for a year - inherit a fortune.
If you want happiness for a lifetime - help someone else.

- Chinese Proverb

How far you go in life depends on you being
- Tender with the Young,
- Compassionate with the Aged,
- Sympathetic with the Striving, and
- Tolerant with the Weak and the Strong,
because some day you will have been all of these.

- George Washington Carver

3 A's?

Our vision is:
Love - through Service to others
Peace – through Reconciliation
Joy – through generous Hospitality.

- Koinonia Mission

If you want others to be happy practice Compassion.
If you want to be happy – practice Compassion.

- The Dalai Lama

Love the earth and sun and animals,
Despise riches, give alms to everyone that asks,
Stand up for the stupid and crazy,
Devote your income and labor to others...
And your very flesh shall be a great poem.

– Walt Whitman

The only people with whom you should try to get even are those
who have helped you

- John E. Southard

People will not give you their hand until they see your heart.
- John Maxwell

People don't care how much you know until they know how
much you care.

- Anonymous

Life is mostly froth and bubble,
but two things stand like stone,
kindness in another's trouble
and courage in your own.

- Princess Diana

We are not held back by the love we didn't receive in the past, but by the love we're not extending in the present.
- Marianne Williamson

Love must be as much a light as it is a flame.
- Henry David Thoreau

You cannot do a kindness too soon, for you never know how soon it will be too late.
- Ralph Waldo Emerson

Dare to be "bothered". Helping others can seem to be a "bother" in time and effort. Do it anyway.
- Dad

Kindness in words creates confidence. Kindness in thinking creates profoundness. Kindness in giving creates love.
– Lao Tzu

3 A's?

Everyone can be great, because everyone can serve.

- Dr. Martin Luther King Jr

Thousands of candles can be lighted by a single candle, and the life of the candle will not be shortened. Happiness never decreases by being shared.

- Buddha

The service we render others is really the rent we pay for our room on earth,

- Sir Wilfred Grenfell

Smiling is Infectious

Smiling is infectious,
you catch it like the flu,
When someone smiled at me today,
I started smiling too.

I passed around the corner
and someone saw my grin.
When he smiled I realized
I'd passed it on to him.

I thought about that smile,
then I realized its worth.
A single smile, just like mine
could travel round the earth.

So, if you feel a smile begin,
don't leave it undetected.
Let's start an epidemic quick,
and get the world infected!

- Author Anonymous

3 A's?

Notes

Record some of your own insights and decisions here

an Attitude of Gratitude

Gratitude is an attitude.
It is the water that nourishes the seeds
that grow into Joy and Contribution.

- Dad

Chapter XV

THANKFULNESS
(Final Approach)

It is said, "What gets measured gets managed." For greater personal development, we must create a personal measure and management tool for our intangibles of:

- Gratitude
- Joy
- Peace of Mind
- Physical Health
- Spiritual Peace
- Sense of Contribution

These measures will be highly subjective and very personal. The effort you put into creating a personal benchmark which allows you to calibrate your current state of mind for these intangibles will be greatly rewarded.

Becoming aware of where your mind is staging allows you to take control and move up your scale through "acting as if".

No one can create this joy, peace of mind, or fulfillment for us. Remember, our first job is to create the mindset and thereby the conditions that allow these to occur. The mindset of Gratitude is a great start.

The author and philosopher, James Allen, advises us to, "Cherish your visions. Cherish your ideals. Cherish the music that stirs in your heart, the beauty that forms in your mind, the loveliness that drapes your purest thoughts, for out of them will grow all delightful conditions, all heavenly environment; of these, if you but remain true to them, your world will at last be built."

Many philosophers have advised that a thankful mind is the one that is the most observant and receptive to external support. Being thankful broadens our focus and illuminates new opportunities. The mental state of gratitude allows us to transmit any condition into a higher state.

Final Approach

The only way to experience the richness of life is to live in an "attitude of Gratitude": to appreciate what you have and what you can give.

- Anthony Robbins

Gratitude isn't a debt to be paid but a key to a treasure chest filled with the fullness of life.

- Michael Josephson

Gratitude unlocks the fullness of life.
It turns what we have into enough, and more.
It turns denial into acceptance, chaos to order, confusion to clarity.

- Michael Josephson

It (gratitude) can turn a meal into a feast, a house into a home, a stranger into a friend.
Gratitude makes sense of our past, brings peace for today, and creates a vision for tomorrow.

- Melody Beattie

How life comes at you today is determined by your past. How you take it is determined by your present.
How you send it forth determines your future. Send it forth with joy.

- Anonymous

I am convinced all of humanity is born with more gifts than we know.

- Richard Buckminster Fuller

Feeling gratitude and not expressing it is like wrapping a present and not giving it.

- William Arthur Ward

The unthankful heart discovers no mercies; but let the thankful heart sweep through the day and, as the magnet finds the iron, so it will find, in every hour, some heavenly blessings!

- Henry Ward Beecher

Expressing gratitude is transformative, just as transformative as expressing complaint.... Expressing gratitude can, indeed, change our way of seeing ourselves and the world.

- Roshi John Daido Loori

What if you gave someone a gift, and they neglected to thank you for it - would you be likely to give them another? Life is the same way. In order to attract more of the blessings that life has to offer, you must truly appreciate what you already have.

- Ralph Marston

The art of acceptance is the art of making someone who has just done you a small favor wish that he might have done you a greater one.

- Russell Lynes

3 A's?

Appreciation can make a day, even change a life. Your willing-ness to put it into words is all that is necessary.

- Margaret Cousins

Each day offers us the gift of being a special occasion if we can simply learn that as well as giving, it is blessed to receive with grace and a grateful heart.

- Sarah Ban Breathnach

You must learn to understand the secret of gratitude. It is more than just so-called virtue. It is revealed to you as a mysterious law of existence. In obedience to it we have to fulfill our destiny.

- Albert Schweitzer

In the end the love you take is equal to the love you make.

- The Beatles

When we are grateful the option of abundance appears and dis-solves the virus of fear.

- Wendy Franklin Muhammed

Abundance is not something we acquire. It is something we tune into.

- Dr. Wayne Dyer

It's impossible to feel grateful and depressed in the same moment.

- Naomi Williams

3 A's?

Notes
Record some of your own insights and decisions here

Luminous beings are we,
not this crude matter.

– Yoda

The most beautiful thing we can experience is the mysterious.
It is the source of all true art and science.

- Albert Einstein

Chapter XVI

SPIRIT
(Refueling)

Spirit and Thankfulness could have easily been the first entries. Gratitude is an energy that fuels all actions and attitudes from Responsibility, to Courage, to Service.

Spirit is the connection to the Powers larger than we are. From cave-dwellers to moon-walkers, most humans have held to the belief that there is a Force and Universal Order that transcends human limitations and understanding. Linking to this Force, for many, is a source of hope, support, connection, and potential transcendence. The belief that one's life has meaning beyond birthing and dying creates a palette and wonder for continual human metamorphosis and discovery. As Pierre Teilhard de Chardin said,

> *We are not physical beings having a spiritual experience, we are spiritual beings having a physical experience.*

Refueling

Integrity is the Key.
Spirit is the Answer.

- Dad

The most beautiful thing we can experience is the mysterious. It is the source of all true art and all science. He to whom this emotion is a stranger, who can no longer pause to wonder and stand rapt in awe, is as good as dead: his eyes are closed.

- Albert Einstein

Spirituality is a domain of awareness.

- Deepak Chopra

In the depth of your hopes and desires
lies your silent knowledge of the beyond;
And like the seeds dreaming beneath the snow
your heart dreams of spring.
Trust the dreams,
for in them is hidden the gate to eternity.

- Khalil Gibran

We need to find God, and He cannot be found in noise and rest-lessness. God is the friend of silence. See how nature – trees, flow-ers, grass- grows in silence; see the stars, the moon and the sun, how they move in silence… We need silence to be able to touch souls.

– Mother Teresa

3 A's?

We can become aware of the miracles within and around us by opening our spiritual eyes. These moments of keen awareness bring us into our essential nature--beings created with miraculous talents to develop and share.

- Steve Brunkhorst

The fact that I can plant a seed and it becomes a flower, share a bit of knowledge and it becomes another's, smile at someone and receive a smile in return, are to me continual spiritual exercises.

- Leo Buscaglia

Faith is not something to grasp, it is a state to grow into.

- Mohandas Gandhi

Just as a small fire is extinguished by the storm whereas a large fire is enhanced by it - likewise a weak faith is weakened by predicament and catastrophes whereas a strong faith is strengthened by them.

- Viktor E. Frankl

I would rather live my life as if there is a God, and die to find out there isn't, than live my life as if there isn't, and die to find out there is.

- George Carlin

There are two ways to live: you can live as if nothing is a miracle; you can live as if everything is a miracle.

- Albert Einstein

3 A's?

Love the animals, love the plants, love everything. If you love everything, you will perceive the divine mystery in things. Once you perceive it, you will begin to comprehend it better every day. And you will come at last to love the whole world with an all-embracing love.

– Fyodor Dostoyevsky

People living deeply have no fear of death.

– Anaïs Nin

To confine our attention to terrestrial matters would be to limit the human spirit.

- Stephen Hawking

3 A's?

I trust that the 19th century English poet, William Dunkerley, will approve of my slight editing of his wonderful poem, "The Way".

The Way

Some men are on the High way,
Some men are on the Low.

And some on the misty, muddy flats below
Go aimlessly to and fro.

Some men choose the High way
Others choose the Low.

And the choice we make
Determines which way our Soul will go.

Notes

Record some of your own insights and decisions here

About the Author

James G. Yarbrough, Jr.

Jim served as a US Air Force pilot, and for the last 25 years, has blended his business career, owning and managing companies engaged in international trade, with international NGO's committed to public service. Jim has lived and worked in five continents and many countries. He is married to Maria Elena Robison of Panama, and together they have three successful adult children.

Thank you again for purchasing this compilation of aphorisms.

A portion of the revenue received will be donated
to two of my favorite charities:

If you would like to learn more about these two great organizations,
please visit their websites at:

www.habitat.org

www.operationsmile.org

Index of Authors

A

Albom, Mitch
American novelist, journalist, columnist
1958–

Ali, Muhammad
American boxer
1942–

Allen, James
British writer
1864–1912

Angelou, Maya
American poet, civil rights activist
1928–

Apollo, Temple of

Arnold, Oren
American editor, freelance writer
1900–1980

B

Ball, Lucille
American actress, comedian
1911–1989

Barry, Dan
American professor
1953–

Basho, Matsuo
Japanese poet
1644–1694

The Beatles
British rock band
1960–1970

Beattie, Melody
American author
1948–

Beecher, Henry Ward
American Protestant clergyman
1813–1887

Bernstein, Leonard
American conductor, composer, author
1918–1990

Bird, Larry
American basketball player
1956–

Blanchard, Ken
American author, management expert
1939–

Boetcker, William J.
American religious leader, speaker
1873–1962

Bounds, E. M.
American Methodist minister, author
1835–1913

Bradshaw, Terry
American football quarterback
1948–

Breathnach, Sarah Ban
American author, spiritualist
1958–

Brinkley, David
American television news anchor
1920–2003

Brown, Les
American big band leader, composer
1912–2001

Buscaglia, Leo
American speaker, writer, professor
1924–1998

Buddha, Gautama
Indian spiritual teacher
c. 563–483 BC

Buddhism
The teachings of Buddha

Bulwer Lytton, E.G.
British politician, poet, playwright, novelist
1803–1873

C

Caddy, Eileen
Irish born spiritual teacher, author
1917–2006

Camara, Dom Helder
Italian Bishop
1909–1999

Camus, Albert
French author, journalist
1913–1960

Carlin, George
American comedian, actor, author
1937–2008

Carlyle, Thomas
Scottish essayist, satirist, historian
1795–1881

Carnegie, Dale
American writer, lecturer
1888–1955

Carver, George Washington
American scientist, botanist, inventor
1864–1943

The Chambers Brothers
American soul music group
1954–1972

Chekov, Anton
Russian writer, playwright
1860–1904

Chopra, Deepak
American Indian physician, writer, teacher
1946–

Churchill, Winston
British statesman, Prime Minister
1874–1965

Cicero
Roman politician, lawyer, orator, philosopher
106 BC–43 BC

Clancy, Tom
American novelist
1947–

Coelho, Pablo
Brazilian novelist, lyricist
1947–

Coffee, Gerald
American Naval Captain, author
1935–

Collier, Robert
American author
1885–1950

Collins, Marva
American educator
1936–

Confucius
Chinese Philosopher
551 BC–479 BC

Conversations With God
A series of books by Neale Donald Walsch
1995–2005

Conway, Peyton
American soldier, Army Chief of Staff.
1864–1955

Cooke, Alfred Alistair
Anglo American journalist, TV personality
1908–

Cooley, Mason
American Aphorist
1927–2002

Courtenay, Bryce
South African/Australian novelist
1933–

Cousins, Margaret
American fiction writer, editor
1905–1996

Covey, Stephen
American author, professional speaker,
1932–

Crowley, Mary
Irish politician
1903–1966

Cummings, E.E.
American poet, essayist, author, playwright.
1894–1962

D

The Dalai Lama
The 14th Dalai Lama, Tenzin Gyatso
1935–

da Vinci, Leonardo
Italian painter, scientist, engineer, inventor
1452–1519

De Angelis, Barbara
American relationship consultant, author
1951–

Dhammapada
Buddhist scripture

Diana, Princess Diana
British Royalty, humanitarian activist
1961–1997

Dickinson, Emily
American poet
1830–1886

Diderot, Dennis
French philosopher, art critic, writer.
1713–1784

Didion, Joan
American novelist, memoirist, essayist
1934–

Disney, Walt
American film producer
1901–1966

Dostoyevsky, Fyodor
Russian novelist, short story writer, essayist
1821–1881

Downs, Hugh
American television broadcaster, host, author
1921–

Drucker, Peter
Austrian writer, management consultant
1909–2005

Durant, William
Irish historian, writer, philosopher, teacher
1885–1981

Dyer, Dr. Wayne
American advocate, author, lecturer.
1940–

E

Edison, Thomas
American inventor, scientist, businessman
1847–1931

Ehrman, Max
American attorney, businessman
1872–1945

Einstein, Albert
German theoretical physicist
1879–1955

Emerson, Ralph Waldo
American essayist, lecturer, poet
1803–1882

Everett, Douglas H.
Canadian lawyer, Senator.
1927–

Ewing, Sam
American baseball player
1949–

F

Farber, Steve
American author, motivational speaker
1959–

Feather, William
American author
1889–1981

Ferrucci, Piero
Italian psychotherapist, philosopher

Finley, Guy
American writer, philosopher, musician
1949–

Firebaugh, Doug
American author

Flaubert, Gustave
French novelist, playwright
1821–1880

Forbes, Malcolm
American publisher, business magnate
1919–1990

Ford, Henry
American industrialist, business magnate
1863–1947

Fowler, Chad
American writer, speaker, teacher

Frank, Anne
German Jewish holocaust victim, diarist
1929–1945

Frankl, Viktor E.
Austrian neurologist, psychiatrist
1905–1997

Franklin, Benjamin
American scientist, writer, politician
1706–1790

Friedman, Milton
American economist, statistician
1912–2006

Friedman, Thomas
American author, columnist
1953–

G

Gandhi, Mahatma
Indian political, ideological leader
1869–1948

Gerber, Michael E.
American author
1936–

Gibran, Kahlil
Lebanese-American poet, philosopher,
1883–1931

Glade, Earle J.
American Mormon missionary, broadcaster
1885–1966

Gladstone, William E.
British Prime Minister
1809–1898

von Goethe, Johann Wolfgang
German poet, novelist, philosopher
1749–1832

Grenfell, Sir Wilfred
British medical missionary
1865–1940

H

Harrison, Elizabeth
American college president, educator, author
1849–1927

Henley, William Ernest
English poet, critic, editor
1849–1903

Herbert, George
English poet, orator, priest
1593–1633

Herman, George "Babe Ruth"
American baseball player
1895–1948

Hesse, Hermann
German Swiss novelist, author, essayist, poet
1877–1962

Hill, Napoleon
American author, journalist, lecturer
1883–1970

Holmes, Oliver Wendell
American physician, professor, author
1809–1894

Holtz, Lou
American coach, sportscaster, author
1937–

Homer
Greek poet
8th century BC

Hoover, Herbert
American President
1874–1964

Hopkins, Tom
American motivational speaker

Hugo, Victor
French poet, playwright, novelist, statesman
1802–1885

Humphrey, Hubert
American Vice President
1911–1978

I

Ingersoll, Robert Green
American political leader
1833–1899

Isaacson, Walter
American author of biographies
1962–

J

Jackson Brown Jr., H.
American author

Jackson Brown, J.
American musician, activist
1948–

James, Clive
Australian essayist, poet, broadcaster
1939–

James, William
American psychologist, philosopher
1842–1910

Jefferson, Thomas
American author, statesman
1743–1826

Joe Dirt
American comedy film, 2001

Jones, Arthur
American inventor
1926–2007

Jong, Erica
American author, teacher
1942–

Josephson, Michael
American speaker, lecturer, law professor
1942–

K

Keith, Kent M.
American author, motivational speaker
1948–

Keller, Helen
American author, political activist, lecturer
1880–1968

Kelly, Matthew
British television presenter, actor
1950–

Kennedy, John F.
American President
1917–1963

Kent, Corita
French artist, educator
1918–1986

Kersey, Cynthia
American author, motivational speaker

Kettering, Charles F.
American inventor, engineer, businessman

King, Coretta Scott
American activist, author
1927– 2006

Kiyosaki, Robert
American businessman, author, speaker
1947–

Knight, Bobby
American basketball coach
1940–

Koinonia Mission

Korbut, Olga
Russian Olympic Gold Medalist gymnast
1955–

Kübler Ross, Elizabeth
Switzerland psychiatrist
1926–2004

L

L'Amour, Louis
American novelist, short story writer
1908–1988

Landry, Tom
American football player, coach
1924–2000

Lao Tzu
Chinese philosopher
Warring States Period, 5th to 4th century BC

Larson, Christian
American New Thought teacher, author
1874–1962

Lasorda, Tommy
American Major League baseball manager
1927–

Levinson, Sam
American humorist, writer, journalist
1911–1980

Lincoln, Abraham
American President
1809–1865

Linkletter, Art
Canadian broadcaster
1912–2010

Lombardi, Vince
American football coach
1913–1970

Loori, John Daido
American Zen Buddhist abbot
1931–2009

Luce, Clare Booth
American playwright, journalist, diplomat
1903–1987

Lynes, Russell
American art historian, photographer, author
1910–1991

M

MacEwan, Norman
British Royal Air Force Commander
1881–1953

Mackay, Harvey
American businessman, columnist.
1932–

Mahfouz, Naguib
Egyptian novelist
1911–2006

Mahoney, David
American soccer goalkeeper
1981–

Maltz, Dr. Maxwell
American cosmetic surgeon
1899–1975

Mandela, Nelson
South African political activist, President
1918–

Mandino, Og
American author
1923–1996

Mansfield, Katherine
New Zealand writer,
1888–1923

Marston, Ralph
American professional football player
1907–

Mason, John
English Army Major, American colonist
1600–1672

Masters, Edgar Lee
American poet, biographer, lawyer
1868–1950

Maxwell, John C.
American author, speaker, pastor
1947–

Meyer, Paul J.
American author, speaker
1928–2009

Moore, Christopher
American novelist
1957–

Moore, Thomas
Irish poet, singer, songwriter, entertainer
1779–1852

Morley, Christopher D.
American journalist, novelist, essayist, poet
1890–1957

Moses, "Grandma Moses"
American folk artist
1860–1961

Murphy, Thomas P.
American businessman
1915–2006

N

Napoleon
Napoleon Bonaparte, French emperor
1769–1821

Nietzsche, Friedrich
German philosopher, poet, composer
1844–1900

Nightingale, Earl
American speaker, author
1921–1989

Nin, Anaïs
French-Cuban author
1903–1977

P

Paddleford, Clementine
American writer
1898–1967

Pascal, Blaise
French mathematician, philosopher
1623–1662

Pavarotti, Luciano
Italian operatic tenor
1935–2007

Peale, Norman Vincent
American author, speaker
1898–1993

Powell, Colin
US Army General, Secretary of State
1937–

Proctor, Bob
American business consultant

R

Rand, Ayn
Russian-American philosopher, writer
1905–1982

Reagan, Ronald
American President, actor
1911–2004

Redmoon, Ambrose
American beatnik, hippie, writer
1933–1996

Rice, Grantland
America sportswriter
1880–1954

Robbins, Anthony
American author, actor, speaker
1960–

"Rocky", Rocky Balboa
1976–2006

Rogers, Will
American actor, comic, columnist
1879–1935

Rohn, Jim
American, author, motivational speaker
1930–2009

Roosevelt, Eleanor
American First Lady, diplomat, activist
1884–1962

S

Saint Jerome
Roman Christian priest
c.341 AD–402 AD

Sartre, Jean Paul
French writer, philosopher
1905–1980

Schopenhauer, Arthur
German philosopher
1788–1860

Schuler, Robert H.
American televangelist, author
1926–

Schuller, Robert
American author, television executive
1954–

Schultz, Charles
American football player
1915–1989

Schwarzenegger, Arnold
Austrian-American actor, politician
1947–

Schwarzkopf, H. Norman
American U.S. Army General
1934–

Schweitzer, Albert
German Alsatian theologian
1875–1965

Seneca, Marcus Annaeus
Roman writer
c. 54 BC–39 AD

Shaw, George Bernard
Irish playwright, critic, political activist
1856–1950

Shinn, Florence Scovel
American artist, book illustrator
1871–1940

Socrates
Athenian philosopher
c. 469 BC–399 BC

Stephenson, Sean
American author, motivational speaker
1979–

Stevenson, Robert Louis
Scottish novelist, poet, travel writer
1850–1894

Stone, W. Clement
American businessman, philanthropist
1902–2002

Dr. Suess
American writer, cartoonist, animator, artist
1904–1991

Swindoll, Charles R.
American pastor, author, educator
1934–

T

Tagore, Rabindranath
Indian (Bengali) polymath
1861–1941

Teilhard de Chardin, Pierre
French palaeontologist, priest, philosopher
1881–1955

Tao
"The Way", a traditional Chinese philosophy

Templeton, John
Anglo-American philanthropist
1912–2008

Teresa, "Mother Teresa"
Catholic nun, charity missionary
1910–1997

Thoreau, Henry David
American author, poet, philosopher
1817–1862

Thurman, Howard
American author, philosopher, theologian,
1899–1981

Tracy, Brian
Canadian author
1944–

Truman, Harry
American President
1884–1972

Twain, Mark
American writer, lecturer
1835–1910

U

The Upanishads
Ancient Vedic text

V

Van Gogh, Vincent
Dutch painter
1853–1890

Viscott, David
American psychiatrist, author
1938–1996

W

Waitley, Denis
American speaker, writer
1933–

Walsch, Neale Donald
American author
1943–

Ward, William Arthur
American writer
1921–1994

Washing, Booker T.
American educator, author
1856–1915

Wattles, Wallace D.
American author, philosopher
1860–1911

Wayne, John
American actor, director, producer
1907–1979

Wesley, John
British preacher, theologian
1703–1791

Wharton, Edith
American novelist, designer
1862–1937

Whitman, Walt
American poet, essayist, journalist
1819–1892

Wilcox, Ella Wheeler
American author, poet
1850–1919

Williamson, Marianne
American author, lecturer
1952–

Wilson, Woodrow
American statesman, President
1856–1924

Wolff, Morris
British actor
1925–1996

Wooden, Coach John
American player, coach
1910– 2010

Y

Yeats, William Butler
Irish poet, playwright
1865–1939

Yoda
A character in the Star Wars films

Z

Ziglar, Zig
American author, motivational speaker
1926–

Zola, Emile
French novelist, playwright, journalist
1840–1902

www.ingramcontent.com/pod-product-compliance
Lightning Source LLC
Chambersburg PA
CBHW071414090426
42737CB00011B/1459